A Model for Calculating Interconnection Costs in Telecommunications

A Model for Calculating Interconnection Costs in Telecommunications

Guidebook prepared by Paul Noumba Um, Laurent Gille,
Lucile Simon, and Christophe Rudelle

 THE WORLD BANK   PPIAF

This guidebook is a publication of the Public–Private Infrastructure Advisory Facility (PPIAF). PPIAF is a multidonor technical assistance facility, aimed at helping developing countries improve the quality of their infrastructure through private sector involvement. For more information on the facility, see the website at www.ppiaf.org.

The findings, interpretations, and conclusions expressed in this guide are entirely those of the authors and should not, in any manner, be attributed to the PPIAF, the World Bank or its affiliated organizations, or to members of its Board of Executive Directors or the countries they represent. Neither PPIAF nor the World Bank guarantees the accuracy of the data included in this publication or accepts responsibility for any consequence of their use. The boundaries, colors, denominations, and other information shown on any map in this report do not imply, on the part of PPIAF or the World Bank Group, any judgment on the legal status of any territory, or the endorsement or acceptance of such boundaries.

In regard to questions concerning this publication, or information on ordering more copies, please refer to the PPIAF website, or contact PPIAF by email at the address below.

PPIAF
c/o The World Bank
1818 H Street
Washington, DC 20433
Fax: 202-522-7466
www.ppiaf.org
Email: info@ppiaf.org

ISBN 0-8213-5671-2

Library of Congress Cataloging-in-Publication Data

Modèle de détermination des tarifs d'interconnexion. English.
    A model for calculating interconnection costs in telecommunications / edited by … [Paul Noumba Um].
        p. cm.
    Includes bibliographical references.
    ISBN 0-8213-5671-2
        1. Telecommunications—Rates—Africa, Sub-Saharan—Mathematical models. 2. Telecommunications—Africa, Sub-Saharan—Costs—Mathematical models. I. Noumba Um, Paul. II. Title.

HE8467.M6313 2003
384.6'4—dc22

                                                                2003067270

Contents

Boxes

Foreword

The tremendous economic and social impact resulting from pervasive, as well as effective, use of information and communication technologies has convinced more and more African governments to embark on the restructuring and progressive liberalization of their telecommunications sectors.

In a liberalized market, a procompetitive regulatory framework is a factor in establishing a level playing field for a favorable environment that encourages greater participation by the private sector. In that respect, establishing a sound interconnection framework that ensures equal treatment, nondiscrimination among market players, and cost-based tariffs is assumed to be the main engine for developing competition in the sector.

Determining interconnection tariffs is a complex and extremely sensitive task. In Africa, the absence of accurate cost information has rendered the situation all the more complex. In fact, some telecommunications regulators resolve interconnection disputes on the grounds of available tariff benchmarking, although these tariffs may not always be relevant.

This guidebook provides a sound methodology to help regulators and telecommunications operators adopt a tariff regime and deal with interconnection disputes on the basis of a rigorous cost model.

Furthermore, it demonstrates the World Bank Group commitment to assist governments in developing the proper enabling environments and effective regulatory institutions, and hence, contribute effectively in mitigating the regulatory risk as perceived by potential investors. Helping newly established regulatory agencies develop their capacity has been underscored as a key pillar of the new World Bank Group Information and Communication Technologies (ICT) strategy (www.worldbank.org/ict).

We sincerely hope that this guidebook and its cost model will be used by telecom regulators and operators to settle interconnection disputes. However, we would urge regulators to customize and expand the cost model to better match their internal needs.

The guidebook consists of six chapters. Chapter 1 introduces the guidebook. Chapter 2 provides an overview of the guidebook. Chapter 3 reviews cost modeling principles for calculating interconnection rates, while chapter 4 illustrates how these principles are integrated in the cost model. Chapter 5 is a user guide and chapter 6 reviews cost modules composing the model and illustrates how interconnection costs are computed.

Mohsen A. Khalil

Acronyms and Abbreviations

ABC	Activity-based accounting	MSC	Mobile switching center
ADM	Add-drop multiplexer	MUX	Multiplexer
BHCA	Business hour call attempts	NRA	National regulatory authorities
BHE	Business hour Erlangs	PDH	Plesiochronous digital hierarchy
BSC	Base station controller	PPIAF	Public–Private Infrastructure
BTS	Base terminal station		Advisory Facility
CS	Central station	RCU	Remote concentrator unit
ECPR	Efficient component pricing rule	RIO	Reference interconnection offer
EU	European Union	SDH	Synchronous digital hierarchy
FDC	Fully distributed costs	TDMA	Time division multiplexing access
GDP	Gross domestic product	TELRIC	Total element LRIC
GICT	Global Information &	TRX	Transmitter/receiver
	Communication Technologies	TS	Terminal station
IS	International switch	TSLRIC	Total service LRIC
IT	Information technology	TSW	Transit switch
LRAIC	Long run average incremental costs	USO	Universal service obligation
LRIC	Long run incremental cost	WACC	Weighted average cost of capital
LS	Local switch	WBI	World Bank Institute

About the Authors

Paul Noumba Um is lead infrastructure specialist, World Bank Institute (WBI), The World Bank Group. Previously, he was regional coordinator for Africa in the policy division of the Communications and Information Technology department.

Laurent Gille is head of the department of economics and social science at École Nationale Supérieure des Télécommunications (ENST) Paris, 46 Rue Barrault, Paris 75013 France. Previously, he was head of the regulation group in BIPE SA.

Lucile Simon and Christophe Rudelle are consultants with BIPA SA – L'Atrium, 6 place Abel Gance, Boulogne Billancourt, 92652 France.

Introduction

Since the past decade, several Sub-Saharan African governments, through technical assistance provided by the World Bank and other donors, have undertaken to reform their telecommunications sectors, by implementing market liberalization policies, privatizing the incumbent public operator, and creating autonomous and independent regulatory bodies. The core objective of these reforms is to significantly improve access, and affordability, to telecommunications services on the basis of the assumption that a more friendly and predictable business environment will attract more private investment. However, the provision of interconnection services, on fair and efficient terms, has rapidly emerged as a main bottleneck.

In fact, new legislation and regulations enacted in Sub-Saharan Africa recognize the interconnection rights ascribed to all telecommunications service providers and network operators. In addition, these regulations also request the incumbent fixed operator to supply interconnection services to new entrants on a fair and competitive basis. Despite the clarity and soundness of the legislative provisions in that respect (cost oriented, nondiscriminatory, fair, and transparent), the number of interconnection disputes has increased, and long-lasting interconnection disputes have discredited the reputation and credibility of new regulatory regimes.

One has to admit, however, that deriving optimal interconnection rates from the principles codified in national laws is tricky in countries constrained by scarce resources (human resources with relevant experience, management and information systems that are unable to provide accurate and comprehensive data, and so forth). As illustrated in table 1.1, interconnection rates are mostly derived from international benchmarking. Although the international benchmarking approach may be a satisfactory starting point, it is not always relevant, since it may not take into account specific country parameters that affect the industry cost structure.

Table 1.1   A Sample of Interconnection Rates

Euro cents/minute	Benin	Burkina Faso	Burundi	Cameroon	Côte d'Ivoire	Mali	Mauritania	Togo
Local	4.5	3.5	3.8	4.0	3.8	3.8	2.6	6.1
Simple transit	4.6	27.8	3.8	8.6	19.8	16.4	7.6	6.1
Double transit	19.8	27.8	3.8	19.8	19.8	16.4	7.6	6.1
Transit	1.8	1.2	3.8					2.3
Mobile termination	19.8	13.4	3.8	22.1	23.7	30.0	7.6	9.9

Source: Data collected from participants of the Access Pricing Workshop held in Ouagadoudou, Burkina Faso, in March 2002.

At the beginning of the sector reform in Africa, in the mid-1990s, it was believed that incumbent fixed operators would hold their dominant position in the long run. However, the recent explosive development of cellular business substantially contradicted that prediction. In most countries, mobile operators connect more subscribers than the fixed service. In a short time, cellular operators have achieved significant market power and are becoming dominant players themselves. Therefore, regulation of interconnection and access pricing should not only focus on calls terminating in the fixed network, but also should consider calls originating or terminating in the mobile networks.

The World Bank Global Information & Communication Technologies (GICT) Department believes that developing a more accurate and robust methodology to assess interconnection rates, based on long-term incremental costs, will support efforts by borrower countries to implement best practice regulation, and would significantly improve the reputation and credibility of national regulatory authorities (NRAs). Our hope is to see this generic cost model customized and expanded by NRAs and be used to solve pervasive interconnection disputes, which have flourished across Africa.

The guidebook includes a CD-ROM that contains the bottom-up cost model. The cost model was developed by BIPE SA[1] under a Public–Private Infrastructure Advisory Facility (PPIAF) grant managed by the World Bank. It builds, to some extent, on a model initially developed by Europe Economics,[2] at the request of the European Commission. However, the proposed model takes into account the specific features characterizing telecommunications development in Africa (embryonic size of the network, predominance of microwave technology for transmission links and limited roll out of fiber-optic cables, rollout of expensive time division multiple access [TDMA] systems to connect rural localities, and limited regulatory capacity), and calculates routing factors, in the light of parameters entered by the user. It generates interconnection rates for fixed-to-fixed, fixed-to-mobile, and mobile-to-fixed calls. Other value-added services are not captured in the attached version but could be easily added by users.

The cost model is available at www.worldbank.org/cit and the Europe Economics model[3] is available at www://europa.eu.int/ISPO/infosoc/telecompolicy/en/Study-en.htm.

The guidebook was prepared by a team led by Paul Noumba Um (World Bank), including Laurent Gille, Lucile Simon, and Christophe Rudelle from BIPE SA (France). The team made use of comments and guidance provided by Antonio Estache and David Satola (World Bank). Daniel Benitez (IDEI, University of Toulouse) reviewed the cost model and provided suggestions for its improvement. We gratefully acknowledge valuable comments provided by participants to the Interconnection Day, which was organized by the GICT Department on April 10, 2003.

We equally wish to express our gratitude for the valuable support offered, throughout this project, by Michele Rajaobelina, Lizmara Kirchner, and Lucy Cueille (World Bank). This exercise could not have been completed without the meaningful collaboration and support provided by telecommunications operators and regulators in the following countries: Burkina Faso, Côte d'Ivoire, Cameroon, Senegal, and Zambia. KC Translations Services LLC revised the English version of the guidebook.

Preliminary Results Provided by the Cost Model

From July 2002 to February 2003, the World Bank GICT Department commissioned BIPE to conduct field visits to Burkina Faso, Cameroon, Côte d'Ivoire, and Zambia. During these visits, workshops were conducted to train regulator and telecom operator staff on how to use the cost model. This section provides an overview of the preliminary findings derived from these visits.

The four countries have implemented telecommunications reforms and established sound regulatory frameworks enabling competition in specified market segments such as the mobile market. Although these countries are not homogeneous, they do, however, reflect a series of commonalities in terms of regulatory framework, market structure, and overall telecommunications development. Interconnection disputes and the urgent need for regulators to ensure their effective and timely settlement were identified as among the primary concerns of private mobile operators. The following table provides an overview of the telecommunications sector situation in these countries.

With the exception of Cameroon, and Côte d'Ivoire, fixed incumbent operators have been granted

Table 1.2 | **Overview of Telecommunications Sectors in Burkina Faso, Côte d'Ivoire, Cameroon, and Zambia**

2001 Data	Burkina Faso*	Côte d'Ivoire	Cameroon	Zambia
Subscribers to the fixed network	60,000	300,000	105,000	105,000
Subscribers to the mobile network	111,145	730,000	510,000	150,000
Number of mobile operators	3	3	2	3

* 2002 data.
Source: BIPE 2003.

mobile licenses. In general, the dominant position of fixed incumbent operators is seriously challenged by the explosive growth observed in the mobile market segment.

In the four countries, interconnection rates were finally decided by regulators in an attempt to settle lengthy interconnection negotiations. In Zambia, interconnection disputes were subsequently brought to the law courts by mobile operators, and are still not settled. In Côte d'Ivoire, following the submission of the revised interconnection rates in 2000 by the fixed incumbent, mobile operators filed complains to the local regulator (ATCI). The arbitration published in

2001 by ATCI was appealed by the fixed incumbent to CTCI, the sector's appeal court for disputes between operators and ATCI. In November 2002, CTCI published its decision on interconnection rates. Neither the ATCI arbitration nor the CTCI appeal decision was based on sound economic analysis.

The preliminary results provided by the cost model during these field visits are summarized below. In Zambia, the fixed incumbent was unable to provide traffic information required to run a cost simulation. In Côte d'Ivoire, arbitration was decided by CTCI, and resulting rates remain higher than the ones recommended after the workshop. In Burkina Faso, the regu-

Table 1.3 | **A Sample of Interconnection Rates Calculated by the Cost Model**

Euro Cents			Burkina Faso		Côte d'Ivoire		Cameroon		Zambia
Fixed Network									
Current Rates									
Local			3.1		9.8		4.0		NA
Simple transit			14.9		9.8		8.5		5
Double transit			14.9		19.8		19.8		NA
Cost Model Rates (with TDMA systems included)									
Local			1.0		3.3		1.7		NA
Simple transit			1.8		4.4		9.6		NA
Double transit			2.4		5.2		12.7		NA
Transit			0.5		0.8		3.1		NA
International transit			2.5		1.0		6.4		NA
Mobile Network									
Current Rates									
Local			9.5		15.2		22.1		5.0
Cost Model Rates	Celtel	Telecel	Telmob	Orange	Telecel	Orange	MTN	Celtel	Telecel
Originating	13	9	8	5.7	7.7	27.2	24.4	14.3	11
Termination	13	9	8	9.8	9.4	27.2	24.4	14.3	11

NA, not applicable.
Notes: The interconnection prices for collection and termination are not theoretically symmetrical in so far as this traffic does not call on the same network elements in a symmetrical way. This lack of symmetry can be taken into account by means of routing factors. However, in the cases of Cameroon and Zambia, we worked with default routing factors that do not discriminate between collection and termination traffic, hence the equality of the results found. We indicated to the operators and regulators that they should refine the calculation of the default routing factors in order to better take into account the real use of the various network elements at traffic collection and termination levels. In reality, the notion of transit corresponds to the difference between double transit and single transit, in a case where a third party operator wants to route traffic on the fixed-line operator's network from one transit zone to another transit zone, while collecting and terminating the traffic itself. For further details, see the model's user guide.
Source: Authors' own calculations.

lator (ARTEL) enacted an interim regulation on interconnection rates following a complaint filed by one of the mobile operators. During the workshops, the discussions and debates were less emotional and were more focused on specific issues related to the relevance of the model assumptions or parameters.

Although it is too early to derive any definitive conclusion from this experience, the empirical results provided by the cost model are quite robust. In Côte d'Ivoire, the interconnection rates generated by the model were below the rates ratified by the regulator for single, double transit, and call termination on the mobile networks. For these services, interconnection is charged above costs, and interconnection providers are extracting monopoly rents. Conversely, local interconnection seems to be cost oriented. Additional actions from the local regulator are therefore needed. In contrast, the simulation in Cameroon provided mixed results. The incumbent's network is not optimized, and costs incurred to provide interconnection services to competitors are therefore abnormally high. Finally, the results show important differences between mobile termination costs in Côte d'Ivoire and Zambia on the one hand, and Cameroon on the other hand. These differences can be explained by substantial investments made by mobile operators in Cameroon to bypass the incumbent, which did not have excess capacity to meet the demands of the mobile operators.

The Limits of the Model

Although the proposed cost model builds on African telecommunication network specificities, it can be applied in non-African environments provided appropriate adaptations are made. The model is easy to use, and requests information that regulators or operators can easily find. However, there remain some limitations. First, the model is designed for "small" networks that do not yet implement complex transit functions or routing algorithms. Second, the model does not seek full optimization when rebuilding the transmission network. More specifically, the model does not optimize the nodes, as the current network topology is kept unchanged ("scorched node" or Brownfield approach). Third, it does not provide a detailed modeling of the cables and duct networks, though it discriminates among different types of geography (urban, suburban, rural) or nature of the trenches (wrapped, ducted, buried). Such a module could be developed by each regulator, although node location optimization may not be critical at the current stage of telecommunications network development in developing countries.

In conclusion, the proposed cost model provides accurate cost proxy estimates when applied to networks with less than 1.5 million main lines and when the incumbent's network topology (number and location of nodes) is optimized or close. As shown in

| Figure 1.1 | **Comparison between Interconnection Prices: Côte d'Ivoire** |

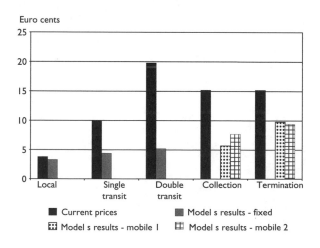

| Figure 1.2 | **Comparison between Interconnection Prices: Cameroon** |

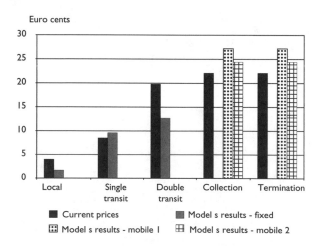

Cameroon, the results obtained when the incumbent's network is underoptimized may be misleading. In a subsequent version of the cost model, an "earth node" module will be added to generate interconnection costs when node location and links are optimized. Therefore, regulators will be able to calculate a bounded interval of interconnection rates. The lower bound will correspond to a configuration of a fully optimized network (nodes and links), while the upper bound will correspond to a partially optimized network (only links are optimized).

Notes

1. BIPE SA can be contacted at: L'Atrium, 6, place Abel Gance, F92652 Boulogne Billancourt Cedex, Tel.: 33 (0)1 46 94 45 22, Fax: 33 (0)1 46 94 45 99, E-mail: Accueil@bipe.fr, http://www.bipe.fr.

2. Europe Economics Research Ltd. (Europe Economics) can be contacted at: Chancery House, 53-64 Chancery Lane, London WC2A 1QU, Tel.: (+44) (0) 20 7831 4717, Fax: (+44) (0) 20 7831 4515.

3. See "Final Report on the Study of an Adaptable Model Capable of Calculating the Forward-Looking, Long-Run Incremental Costs of Interconnection Services for EU Member States" (April 2000), prepared for the European Commission by Europe Economics. This study resulted in the production of a model spreadsheet in MS-Excel format [EN, 4 Mb] (with a voluminous user guide), which is described in the main report [EN, 440 kb] and an executive summary [EN, 65 kb] (both available here as Adobe Acrobat *.pdf files).

2 | Guidebook Overview

Interconnection negotiations and settlements are among the main regulatory issues to reckon with in regard to the development of competition in the telecommunications sector in African countries. Although the majority of legislation includes provisions ensuring the interconnection rights for new entrants and sets cost orientation principles for determining the interconnection rates, only a few regulators are equipped to effectively implement these regulations in practice. Regulators do not have relevant cost information that would allow for effective arbitration of interconnection disputes. Moreover, regulators are not equipped to assess the cost orientation of interconnection rates proposed by fixed incumbents. Hence, they are ill equipped to ratify reference interconnection offers.

Furthermore, it is difficult to replicate cost models developed for more advanced economies in Africa. African networks are small in size and quite spread out. They rely on specific architectures and technologies to reconcile their small market size in volume to the scattered habitat. Transmission links are mostly over microwave technology, and the roll out of fiber-optic systems remains limited to urban centers.

It is in this context that the World Bank contracted BIPE to develop a cost model that captures specificities prevailing in Africa and that could be easily replicable. The model belongs to the bottom-up, long run incremental cost (LRIC) models family, and determines interconnection rates by calculating the costs incurred by an efficient African network operator using the best available technologies. Considering the tremendous development of mobile communications in Africa, the model also calculates the interconnection cost for fixed-to-mobile calls, and conversely.

In general, the model requires the entry of substantial amount of information characterizing the networks that are interconnecting (topology, architecture principles and rules, traffic matrix and patterns, costs elements, and so forth). To palliate the frequent gaps in the information systems, the model proposes default values that the user could consider if needed. This applies mainly to the routing factors, which are rarely documented in most countries.

The overall objective is to provide regulators and operators with a decision tool that can *enhance common understanding and cooperation* in dealing with a sensitive subject. The next sections briefly present the cost modeling principles and the user guide and review the cost model structure.

Cost Modeling Principles

Nobody could envisage dynamic competition in the telecommunications market without the actual enforcement of the interconnection regulations. Without interconnection, competing operators will be obliged to duplicate onerous infrastructure, and consumers would have to subscribe to connections to different operators' networks. Conversely, with an effective interconnection regime, a seamless communication system is more likely to develop, enabling consumers to contract the service with whichever supplier, and be ensured of receiving all incoming calls, from wherever they originate. Nonetheless, the interconnection regime has to be implemented with market liberalization in view; and this calls for free negotiation and contracting. Hence, interconnection agreements have to be freely negotiated in line with regulations. That key principle—as it is applied—opens the door to abuse and strategic behavior from the operator enjoying a dominant market position. Fixed incumbent operators are likely to enjoy a strategic comparative size advantage (number of subscribers) when the market is opened up to competition, which can distort or hamper the development of competition. Safeguards are, therefore, needed to protect new entrants from these anticompetitive behaviors; hence, regulators are mandated by law to ratify reference interconnection offers submitted by incumbents. It is also required that they ratify agreements negotiated by the parties. In so doing, regulators must not only make sure that the agreements are entirely in compliance with existing regulations but they must also check their consistency with the guiding principles, such as interconnection rates cost orientation. In checking compliance with the cost-orientation principle, regulators need to access relevant and accurate cost information to motivate their decisions. However, assessing the cost orientation also requires an ability to assess the way costs for interconnection services are formed and distributed.

This is a complex and cumbersome task. Indeed, a telecommunications operator manages a complex business. It rolls out networks using different technologies and investment layers spread out over time. It offers a portfolio of services, which are interdependent and call on the same productive resources. Furthermore, some of the services are sold on a retail basis (in the final market) while others, such as interconnection services, are sold to other operators forming a wholesale range of products. In such a context, assessing or identifying costs incurred by each category of service requires the implementation of a sophisticated *cost allocation management and information system*.

Economists have proposed various cost allocation methodologies. Some are based on the operator's accounting and involve allocating historical costs to different services according to criteria prescribed by the regulators. Others estimate costs by reconstituting the networks on the basis of currently available technologies. It is generally admitted that the latter are the most appropriate for estimating interconnection services costs. LRIC methodology estimates the costs incurred, while offering a subset of services. The costs considered are those that would be avoided if these services were not offered.

For estimating the cost of the interconnection services, the selected increment comprises network elements belonging to the core network, that is, those shared among all the network's users, excluding network elements dedicated to end users.

The proposed cost model takes into account the specific nature of African networks and has several features:

- A low number of main lines spread out, however, over large territories.
- Traffic concentrated over a small number of network nodes.
- Transit function almost nonexistent, and low capacity of the transmission network, which relies merely on microwave technology.
- Predominance of rural concentration systems that use TDMA-type radio systems.
- The presence of domestic satellite networks.

These specific features are taken into account in the model, and rural radio concentrators are integrated in the increment.

The cost model takes into account six types of nodes and five types of links between these nodes, as summarized in the following table:

Table 2.1	Typology of Nodes and Links in a Telecommunications Network

Nodes	IS	TS	LS	RCU	CS	TS
IS						
TS	to IS	TS-LS	TS-LS			
LS			TS-LS	RCU-LS	(Local link)	
RCU						
CS						CS-TS
TS						

IS, international switch; TS, terminal station; LS, local switch; RCU, remote concentrator unit; CS, central station.

The cost model assumes the existence of two transit levels: international switch (IS) and domestic transit, which are often not implemented in practice. The transit functions are often performed by the local switches (LSs), which are also used to connect subscribers directly or indirectly through remote concentrator units (RCUs). Finally, TDMA technology radio concentrators, characterized by central stations (CSs) and terminal stations (TSs), are widely used to connect remote rural localities to the fixed telephone network.

The cost modeling assumes that costs are:

- **Long-term**—meaning that all the cost components are variable.
- **Forward looking**—implying that the model considers current costs and not historic costs.
- **Efficient**—this implies that the model takes into account the best available technology. This is done without modifying the network topology. In this case, the cost model retains the scorched node approach.
- **Economic**—not accounting costs. For instance, the model converts investment costs into constant equivalent annuities.
- **Bottom-up**—this implies rebuilding the network according to the previous principles.
- Computed per minute.

The cost model is Excel based and includes 21 spreadsheets, 7 of which can be accessed via an interface provided in the Menu sheet. For fixed networks, the model calculates interconnection costs for local, single transit, double transit, and international transit calls. For mobile networks, the model calculates interconnection costs for both terminating and originating calls.

User Guide

The user guide is intended to facilitate the use of the model by staff from regulatory agencies and telecommunications operators.

After selecting a working language (English or French), the user is requested to provide generic parameters defining the network's configuration, architecture, and topology.

The user enters in the blue boxes parameters characterizing the network's configuration in terms of size, architecture, topology.

The parameters describing functionality shared by several networks are filled in by default values. The user can modify these values whenever needed. Two situations are possible:

- Default values are not calculated values and are filled in light green boxes. In this case, the user can modify these values.
- The default values are calculated from the user's inputs and are filled in table format on the right of blank light blue cells. In case the user wants to proceed with default values, then he/she should avoid filling in alternative values.

Once all of the required information is entered or validated, the user can view the results presented in subsequent tables.

- The first table gives the cost per minute of various network elements (nodes and links).
- The second table gives interconnection services costs as follows:
  - The first line provides the average interconnection costs resulting from selected routing factors.
  - The second line supplies the interconnection costs with or without factoring in TDMA system costs. These costs are compared with European best practice rates provided in euros.
  - Finally, the table translates average costs obtained in tariffs according to the pricing structure in force (depending on time or day).
- Similar simplified tables are provided for cost of terminating or originating calls from mobile networks.

The user can refine certain assumptions and conduct a sensitivity test. This can be done for six preselected variables:

- Traffic level at peak time (as a percentage of the overall traffic).
- Total length of trenches: variation by percentage.
- Proportion of staff dedicated to the core network functions (maintenance, operation, and so forth).
- Employee average annual cost.
- Markup to the equipment capital cost incurred by the operator (this is a proxy reflecting exogenous factors that increase capital cost).
- The proportion of debt in the total capital structure.

The user can print a report including the simulation results. Similarly, the user can save the sensitivity test modifications.

The Model

The model is described in greater detail in the third section of this guidebook. The overall logic of the model is simple.

- The model begins with a nomenclature of network elements (nodes and links).
- Each service uses these elements in different proportions. The routing factors represent the average number of times a given element is used by the service considered. The model then calculates the total load supported for each network element.
- The model calculates the size of network elements (transmission elements) within the framework of the selected topology.
- The model adds up all corresponding network element costs and calculates the per-minute cost for each network element.
- Finally, the model calculates the interconnection costs on the basis of the routing factors.

The network is considered to be made up of network elements, namely, nodes and links. These elements convey interconnection traffic throughout the network. This implies the mobilization of network elements according to the complexity of the interconnection service requested.

Furthermore, the model calculates the investment cost and also the cost of operation and maintenance incurred by these network elements. These costs are distributed over four components.

	Investment costs	Operating costs
Attributable costs		
Common costs		

Common costs are expressed as a percentage of the attributable costs. The percentage is usually decided by the regulator and is to some extent arbitrary. The attributable costs are the costs directly caused by the interconnection service and would have been avoided by the provider. They consist of operating and investment costs. The operating costs are composed of two terms:

- Maintenance and operating cost related to the network element (spare parts, equipment section of preventive and corrective maintenance, energy consumed).
- Staff costs related to operation and maintenance activities.

For small but spread-out networks, staff costs can hardly be appraised as a percentage of the investment costs. This is, indeed, a difficult task. The model calculates the number of staff needed to efficiently operate the network and derives salary costs accordingly. The staff cost is then distributed among different network elements according to parameters specified by the user.

Similarly, the investment costs are calculated by considering the estimated volume of traffic to be handled by each network element at peak hour. The size of each network element is accordingly derived using engineering procedures. For each network element, the model calculates the investment cost incurred and generates an investment annuity. Operating and non-attributable costs are then allocated to it to obtain a global cost per minute for each element. For each service, relevant costs per minute for the network element are added up to obtain the interconnection cost. The latter value is adjusted using the gradient of retail prices to derive the interconnection rate.

The model calculates the interconnection costs over two stages.

- First, the model determines the size of the switching elements. Switching elements are considered to be the nodes of the network. Their investment costs depend on the switching system BHE (business hour Erlangs transformed into 2 megabytes per second [Mbps]) and the number of subscribers connected.
- Second, the size of the links connecting network's nodes is calculated. The model differentiates the infrastructure and transmission layers:
  - The transmission layer enables the user to design the electronic transmission equipment by choosing and sizing the capacity of the most appropriate technology to be rolled out (synchronous digital hierarchy [SDH] rings, plesiochronous digital hierarchy [PDH] technology).
  - The infrastructure layer enables the determination of the links' substratum or the physical elements that will support the transmission link: trenches for fiber-optic cables, microwave towers and masts, and satellite earth stations.

The trenches are broken down by geo-type (urban, suburban, and rural) corresponding to various burying techniques (wrapped trench, ducted, fully buried). The microwaves are characterized by the nature of their mass (light, medium, or heavy).

The links are sized by the traffic carried at peak hour expressed in megabit per second (Mbit/s). The transmission link size is determined, to enable normal flow of traffic expected from switching centers and leased lines connected to them. Certain infrastructure elements are shared by different categories of traffic; this is particularly applicable to SDH rings in the access network. The model enables such costs to be shared. For example, SDH rings in the access network will be used to carry core network traffic flow and the access network traffic.

The model comprises 21 sheets organized as follows:

- One menu sheet.
- Twelve sheets forming the core of the model, as described below.
- Four sheets for the mobile networks.
- One sheet to conduct the sensitivity analysis.
- Three specific management sheets (two sheets for publishing the fixed-line and mobile reports, and one sheet to manage the two languages and the default values).

The 12 sheets forming the core of the model are:

- Four sheets for assumptions and parameters enabling the configuration of the network.

- One sheet for calculating the peak load traffic and determining the network's elements size.
- Two sheets for determining the transmission and infrastructure size.
- Three sheets to calculate the network element costs (switching, transmission, and infrastructure).
- One sheet for summing up the total interconnection costs (including the shared costs) and calculating the interconnection costs per minute and per element.
- One sheet to present the results.

Figure 2.1 below summarizes the cost model architecture.

In conclusion, this cost model is a tool provided to regulators and operators to help them:

- Develop a better understanding of the interconnection costing and economics.
- Determine economic-oriented interconnection rates for terminating and departing traffic from, or to, fixed and mobile networks.
- Ratify crucial assumptions pertaining to traffic demand, network optimization, and cost allocation between final and intermediary services.
- Report on the benchmarking exercise, for the ratification of the above mentioned assumptions. *Instead of benchmarking interconnection rates, the regulator should instead focus on benchmarking key cost drivers.*
- Better identify indicators to be monitored, on a regular basis, by the regulator.

Figure 2.1 | Cost Model Architecture

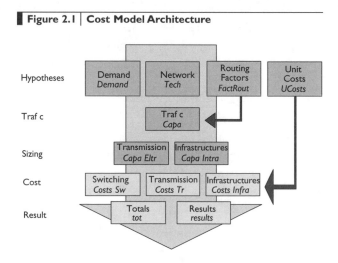

3 | Cost Modeling Principles

Regulation of Interconnection

Since the past decade, the majority of African countries have adopted legislation opening up their telecommunications market, or certain segments of it, to competition. The mobile communications segment was opened up to competition, with two to five mobile operators authorized to commercialize their services. In regard to fixed-line networks, the scope of competition remained limited as temporary exclusivity periods were accordingly granted to incumbent fixed operators before or after their privatization.

In parallel, independent or autonomous regulatory bodies were established in the majority of African countries with the mandate to establish a level and competitive playing field. The right to interconnect was included in various national laws, and national regulators were authorized to effectively enforce its implementation. As expected, regulating interconnection has been one of their main activities. To sum up, the key cross-cutting questions are: (a) Which firms are subject to interconnection rules? (b) What network components are subject to the rules? (c) On what terms can these specific components be shared with competitors? (d) What is the most appropriate term for interconnection contracts? (e) How should the network owners be compensated for interconnection to, and re-use of, their embedded systems?

Implementing interconnection regulations raises multifaceted issues. First, there are technical-related considerations that supersede the effective implementation of interconnection agreements. Are interconnec-tion demands presented by new entrants reasonable? If so, can they be met by the incumbent in a reasonable time frame? Second, the interconnection agreements are assumed to be freely negotiated, as with any other commercial contracts, although they cannot become effective unless approved by the regulator. Are parties likely to reach a fair agreement? If so, how much time should be given to them to reach such agreements? Is the regulator well equipped to review and ratify agreements resulting from private negotiations? Whenever negotiations fail, is the regulator equipped to effectively arbitrate ensuing disputes? What should the procedure be, and what should the appeal procedure be? There are laws stipulating that interconnection tariffs must be cost oriented to ensure productive efficiency. In practice, newly created regulators are ill equipped to perform that role. Field experience also shows that most interconnection disputes are related to rates, highlighting the overall importance of the economic dimension of interconnection pricing. The remainder of this guidebook treats that dimension.

Essential Facilities

Normally, at an early stage of competition development, the incumbent will enjoy a "Stackelberg first move advantage," and will accordingly be considered to be a dominant player. In such a situation, because the incumbent controls access to inputs that new entrants need in order to compete, and can prevent or hamper competition development in downstream markets, there is a need for specific regulations. As a result, the access to these facilities must be regulated. The essential facilities concept refers to those facilities owned or controlled by one of the players, and whose duplication is too costly and uneconomical for new entrants. Essential facilities should therefore be mutual or shared resources, and the need to ensure equal access is straightforward in certain infrastructure sectors as we illustrate here.

Let us assume that there are two airlines in country A. Airline X was the only provider of public air transport service before the government decided to liberalize the market. In the aftermath of air transport liberalization, the government licensed a new airline Y. Prior to the liberalization, airline X was operating 50 routes from the main airport built and owned by the company. To compete with X, airline Y needs to develop its airport or negotiate access to airline X's airport. What would be the outcome of the competition? It is likely that airline Y's capacity to compete with X will be seriously undermined unless it gains fair access to the airport facility controlled by X. In conclusion, the new legislation that enacted the liberalization of the airline market must also ensure fair access to the airport facilities controlled by X. Then, the question becomes how to set the terms for providing and regulating this access.

Obviously, operations and airport ownership should be unbundled to allow fair competition between airlines. Consequently, airport infrastructures are usually owned by the state or its representative while the management of the facility is often delegated to a commercial entity. Unbundling ownership and operation of the airport facility hence allows for the establishment of a level playing field for airline service provision. Of course, further regulations are needed to ensure that all licensed airlines have equal access to air transport services. In the absence of such a regulatory framework, each new airline will have to run a private airport, or be extremely dependent on facilities owned and managed by other competing airlines, hence limiting the development of competition.

Similarly to the airline industry example discussed above, some components of the fixed telecommunication network owned and operated by the incumbent can be considered as being essential facilities, at least during the early development stage of competition. Any failure to provide new entrants access to these facilities

drastically limits the scope of competition. Indeed, in the absence of an interconnection regulatory framework, new entrants would have no other alternative than to roll out their own local loop network in order to reach existing telephone consumers. Consequently, consumers would need to subscribe to as many service providers as possible, and the overall social value of the telephone system would be suboptimal.

Pricing of Essential Facilities

Although interconnection is a mandatory obligation embodied in national regulations, concluding and managing interconnection agreements are generally left to concerned parties, as are other commercial agreements.[1] Consequently, the obligations mandated by legislation and regulations are considerably weakened when the parties' objectives differ significantly. It is, therefore, important that regulations provide sound safeguard measures protecting the most vulnerable players from anticompetitive practices by the incumbent. During the early stage of competition, the incumbent's survival does not depend on fair access to competitors' networks. The survival of new competitors, however, is highly dependent on the terms of access to the incumbent's network and customers. During, the interconnection agreement negotiations, incumbents will likely charge high prices for access to their networks, while entrants will seek cheaper prices. Incumbents will also try to delay the provision of interconnection services, as long as possible, to competitors. In other words, the regulator's role is crucial in deciding fair access terms.

Specific regulations are needed, and are justified, whenever one of the market players enjoys a dominant position. However, in an extremely rare situation in which there is no dominant player, and assuming that all new entrants have sound and mutual interests in accessing each other's network at competitive terms, enforcing specific interconnection regulations may be needless. Nonetheless, the most common situation is when one of the players dominates some market segments, but not necessarily all of them. In that case, the dominant player finds no incentive in facilitating the conclusion of fair interconnection agreements.

It is essential to spell out dominance criteria, as clearly as possible, and to outline the obligations of the dominant player. The new European regulatory package (2002) specifies that "an undertaking shall be deemed to have significant power if, either individually or jointly with others, it enjoys a position of economic strength affording it the power to behave, to an appreciable extent, independently of competitors, customers and ultimately consumers. Where an undertaking has significant market power on a specific market, it may also be deemed to have significant market power on a closely related market, where the links between the two markets are such as allow the market power held in one market to be leveraged into the other market, thereby strengthening the market power of the undertaking."[2]

In practice, controlling a market share of greater than 25 percent is often considered as being in a dominance situation.[3] In general, it is recommended to refer to any relevant jurisprudence that national competition commissions or authorities would have established in that area. As a result, fixed telecommunications incumbent operators would be rightly considered as being powerful or dominant operators. Whenever an operator is dominant or powerful, it is more likely to implement tariff discrimination, hence distorting competition. It is therefore essential to ensure that interconnection services are provided on a nondiscriminatory basis. Interconnection services provided to new entrants should be identical, in terms of quality, technical conditions, and rates to similar services that an incumbent would be providing to its own affiliates.[4]

Regulating interconnection agreements implies that the regulator be appropriately staffed and equipped with a variety of regulatory tools that make it possible to:

- Effectively enforce the accounting separation principle or the unbundling of regulated activities from the competitive ones.
- Ensure that interconnection rates are nondiscriminatory.[5]
- Publish a detailed reference interconnection offer (RIO), including the description of relevant offers broken down into network elements as demanded by the market, and complemented by the corresponding modalities, conditions, and prices.
- Ratify interconnection reference offers submitted by dominant operators according detailed procedures.

- Ratify the terms and conditions of negotiated interconnection agreements.
- Effectively arbitrate interconnection disputes.

Cost Orientation

Nondiscrimination and transparency are not the only obligations imposed on dominant operators. Interconnection rates are also required to be cost oriented. There are two ways for competition to blossom in the telecommunications industry. One way is to support infrastructure-based competition. According to that way, policies and regulations are developed with incentives to promote investments in infrastructure. The rationale in this strategy is that without affordable infrastructure, competition in service provision will remain limited. It is therefore important to support the development of alternative infrastructure providers; this will make the best possible use of technological innovations and will lower entry costs to service providers. The second way is to support service-based competition. According to that way, policies and regulations should be developed with incentives to promote investments in service provision that maximize the load factor of existing infrastructure.

Regulation of input prices is justified whenever there is a risk of substantial anticompetitive practices. Input prices can be priced at excessively high levels or can be priced at overly low levels. In both cases, competition is limited or constrained, either downstream or upstream. However, "the imposition of a price control by national regulatory authorities should not have a negative effect on long-term competition, nor discourage investment in different infrastructures. The national regulatory authorities should take into account the investments made by operators providing these inputs, factoring in the risks incurred accordingly."[6]

In practice, *the cost orientation principle does not mean selling at marginal cost. It is about determining the average cost incurred by an efficient operator using the best available technology.* Consequently, the above-mentioned average cost incorporates possible economies of scale and scope achieved by the operator providing the input. The overall objective is, therefore, to ensure that input prices *reflect the industry productive efficiency frontier.*

To ensure the orientation toward costs, there are two main approaches:

- The first approach relies on benchmarking input prices in similar or comparable environments. This approach contains a serious shortfall. In general, economic conditions differ from one country to another, and differences cannot always be explained by market factors. Some of the differences could just be related to the geography or other specific socioeconomic conditions. Consequently, this approach only provides rough estimates of possible cost frontiers. Regulators should refrain from relying excessively on benchmarking to set interconnection rates.

- The alternative approach is analytical and reviews the cost structure of the regulated operator against the one provided by an efficient operator. Because the operator provides a broad range of services, it is important to be able to differentiate costs according to their relevance to the specific input considered.

To ensure the cost orientation of interconnection rates submitted by dominant operators, *the regulator must build and enhance its knowledge with respect to the industry cost frontier and cost drivers*. The next section further develops the cost allocation methodologies and highlights their relevance and limitations.

Cost Determination Methodologies

For multiproduct firms, determining the cost incurred to produce a specific product or service is a delicate and complex exercise. With the limitations that apply, this section presents the different methodologies that could be used to assess a multiproduct firm cost structure.

The Generic Costs Borne by a Multiproduct Firm

Figure 3.1 illustrates the complexity of a multiproduct firm cost structure. It is assumed that the firm manufactures five products (A, B, C, D, and E). The overall total cost incurred by the firm is also known. The issue, therefore, is to determine the total cost incurred in producing each product. How should the unit cost per product be determined? To begin with, it is important to define the following concepts:

Direct costs or directly attributable costs are expenses that are incurred when producing a specific service or a series of services or products. In other terms, direct costs attributed to product A will cease to exist if product A is no longer manufactured or pro-

duced by the firm. Consequently, these expenses are tied to the production of a specific service or product and should not exist if that production is stopped. Direct costs can be fixed or variable.

Joint costs are generated by a family of services or products (for example, buildings costs for a telephone firm). From an economic viewpoint, joint costs are costs incurred in fixed proportions[7] every time a service or a product belonging to the same family is produced by the firm. For example, a telephone company incurs joint costs whenever it conveys a local, interurban, or international call.

Common costs are shared by all the services or products of the company (for example, the fixed costs of acquiring licenses). Common costs include the remainder of the costs that are not directly attributable or joint, and which are incurred by the firm.

In conclusion, summing up joint and common costs boils down to the total shared costs incurred by the firm. These costs can be attributed to services or products manufactured by the firm using more or less arbitrary criteria. However, whenever shared costs can be attributed in a nonarbitrary way, reflecting the causality factor, they are referred to as *indirectly attributable costs*. Conversely, whenever the attribution can only be arbitrary, it is referred to as *nonattributable costs*.

Figure 3.1 | The Costs of a Multiproduct Firm: An Example for Five Products

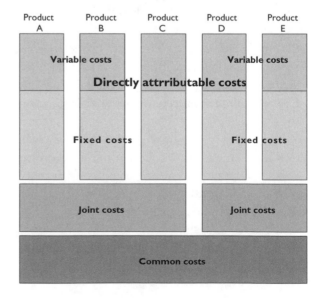

Within *directly attributable costs*, it is important to differentiate fixed from variable costs as follows:

Fixed costs represent the proportion of the firm's expenses that does not depend on, or vary with, the activity of the firm. Fixed costs include production capacity costs and other preinvestment expenses incurred when preparing the launch of the firm's activities. In the event there is a major variation of the firm's activities, the fixed costs component will also vary as a result of the capacity adjustment. However, these adjustments are not necessarily below specified thresholds. From an economic viewpoint, fixed costs are assumed to be independent of the volume of production and are borne by the firm even if it is not operating. Whenever the firm's activities are shut down, some of the fixed costs incurred by the firm become sunk costs. Sunk costs are considered to be nonrecoverable after the firm's activities cease.

Variable costs are closely related to the level and the development of the firm's production and marketing operations. When some operations are halted, the corresponding variable expenses disappear. Conversely, when operations develop, variable costs also move in the same direction. Variable costs include raw material costs, labor costs, other intermediary input costs, as well as variable marketing costs (delivery expenses, brokerage, commissions, allowances). Variable costs are not strictly proportional to the development of the activity because of the evolution characterizing production factors or technology innovation. For instance, if the raw material costs vary proportionally to production, that is not the case with salary costs.

The sum of the fixed costs, the variable costs, the joint costs, and the common costs gives the total production cost or global cost. The global cost or total production cost is directly related to the production volume (total cost increases with production increase). However, in the presence of scale economies, the unit cost drops as production increases. Whenever scope economies are present, it is economically more efficient to have only one firm serving the market than to have several competing firms.

Two fundamental cost concepts yield from the total cost definition recalled above: the average cost and the marginal cost.

Average cost is the unit cost obtained by dividing the total cost by the number of units produced. The average cost function will decrease as production increases up to a threshold beyond which it then increases (at least in the short term) with the output. The average total cost corresponds to the sum of the variable average costs and the average fixed costs.

Marginal cost is the total cost variation resulting from a variation of the firm's production. Marginal cost is defined by economists as the incremental cost resulting from the production of an additional unit (or cost of the last unit produced). A more formal definition is given by the first derivative of the total cost function relative to the produced quantity.

Average and marginal costs are basic concepts in economics, and the definitions given above hold for monoproduct firms. In summary, it is important to recall that marginal cost represents the theoretical bottom cost that a firm has to recover in the short run.

These definitions are slightly modified for a multiproduct firm. In fact, the total costs for a firm producing several goods depend on the quantities and the proportions of goods produced. It is therefore important to differentiate two polar situations: (a) proportions of produced goods do not change; (b) proportions of produced goods do change. The concepts of radial and incremental cost are then used to refine marginal and average costs.

Average radial cost. Whenever the family of goods produced by the firm remains unchanged during the production cycle, it is more appropriate to use the concept of the average radial cost instead of average cost (that is, with a constant proportion of products).

Average incremental cost. Whenever there is a change in the composition or proportion within the family of goods produced by a firm, it is appropriate to use the concept of average incremental cost. The average incremental cost is defined as the average cost associated with a product or a group of products among those manufactured by the firm. The average incremental cost for a product group usually decreases with the increase in the number of product groups (scope economies).

In theory, the marginal, radial, and incremental costs refer solely to the variable component of the cost function. Pricing at marginal cost does not enable the firm to recover the fixed cost. This situation occurs in an industry in which scale and scope economies prevail. One way to solve this problem is to use long-term incremental average costs, as all costs are then variables. However, joint and common costs still have to be financed. Other important cost concepts exist, but we do not discuss them here. Instead, we refer the reader to more advanced economics textbooks.[8]

The cost typology, discussed above, has been simplified on purpose to illustrate issues and problems pertaining to cost-allocation methodologies when dealing with a multiproduct firm. Conversely, the presentation does not reflect the refined cost allocation criteria found in most recent economic literature.

Economic Criteria for Assessing Costs

Taking into account the economic dimension of the various costs categories, as discussed above, entails a better understanding and definition of cost allocation criteria.

The difference between fixed and variable costs is time related. Generally, fixed costs are long term, in the sense that they reflect expenses incurred by the firm to develop capacity and meet its production objectives. Conversely, variable costs are directly related to the day-to-day operations of the firm; hence, they are short term. However, in the long run, even fixed costs are variables. It is therefore possible to reconcile cost accounting analysis to the economic analysis.

NOTIONS OF ECONOMIC COST. The notion of economic cost involves bringing a series of costs spread out over time back to one base year. Adding up all of these costs does not make it possible to measure their economic importance. As such, if we have an income amount Q in year 0, it would be expected that if this amount were invested according to market conditions (interest rate i), it would yield an income $Q*$ such that $Q* = Q \times (1 + i)$ in year 1, and $Q* = Q \times (1 + i)^2$ in year 2, and $Q* = Q \times (1 + i)^n$ in year n, etc.

Conversely, if one intends to spend an income amount D in year n, that implies he or she should, today, have an income equivalent to $D/(1 + i)^n$ today. A sound measurement of a series of expenses with different time occurrence requires discounting the expenses (that is, dividing the expenses in year n by the

$(1 + i)^n$ before adding them. Above, i represents the cost of capital, that is, the cost applying to resources borrowed from the financial market or resources provided by the shareholders in terms of equity.

We also refer to the following:

- **Total discounted cost,** which is given by [the initial investment[9]] − [the resale value in the discounted terminal year] + [discounted operating costs].

- **Economic cost or average discounted cost**, which is the constant annuity equivalent to the discounted current cost.

- **Discounted marginal cost** for year n, in the absence of a resale value, is equal to the operating costs. If the resale value is not 0, it is the sum of the operating costs and gap between the discounted resale value in year $n - 1$ and resale value in year n.

TRENDS ON COST DYNAMIC EVOLUTION. **Historical cost** is the cost value entered in the firm's books (purchasing cost or production cost). This cost obviously cannot represent the real cost of the asset at the end of several years for a series of reasons, including wear, obsolescence, depreciation of the currency, and aging.

Forward-looking, long-term cost: Contrary to historical cost, forward-looking cost relies on the best available technologies, assuming that the firm's production cycle is globally at optimum.

As a general rule, for a company producing several outputs, provided that it is less expensive to jointly produce all the outputs than to produce them separately, the total cost for producing one output is lower in a joint production structure than in a stand-alone production. Otherwise, it would be in the company's interest to produce these different outputs separately. Joint and common costs, therefore, illustrate economies of scope, which the industry production structure entails. However, allocating these costs among products remains a difficult and complex task.

There are several methodologies in regard to allocation of joint and common costs. However, none of these methodologies provides a satisfactory solution. Depending on the methodology used, the resulting allocation is biased by the arbitrariness embodied in each criterion. In general, we look for a cost distribution that avoids cross-subsidization among services or products to the greatest extent possible. As discussed in the box below, the concept of cross-subsidization also has several definitions, depending on the context.

There are clear-cut differences in the way the allocation of joint and common costs is handled by various methodologies. Four main cost allocation methodologies are available. Some are cost allocation methods in the strict sense of the term, while others are pricing methods from which allocation principles are derived. The four methodologies are:

1. The fully distributed costs (FDC) methodology.
2. The efficient component pricing rule (ECPR) methodology.
3. The Ramsey-Boiteux and Laffont-Tirole methodology, which rely on demand-price elasticity.
4. Long-term incremental costs (LRIC) methodology.

None of the above methodologies is fully satisfactory. All of them build on sound economic rationale, and can be criticized or defended depending on one's point of view. The cost model proposed herein builds on the long-term incremental costs methodology, which will be developed later.

The FDC methodology records the expenses incurred by a firm and allocates them to respective products based on the causality principle. In that methodology, a cost breakdown procedure is used that groups costs by nature, function, and, according to an intertwined nomenclature, hierarchy. This approach relies heavily on the availability of reliable accounting information, which is usually generated by activity-based accounting (ABC) systems. Furthermore, the allocation of joint and common costs is done using arbitrary distribution keys.

There are two families of LRIC models: (a) top-down LRIC and (b) bottom-up LRIC.

Top-down LRIC is essentially an ABC methodology. Top-down LRIC models derive incremental costs by summing up the costs that can be directly attributed to the service and adding a markup that covers a proportion of joint and common costs. The markup is determined with the help of arbitrary distribution keys. Therefore, the resulting cost is more backward oriented than forward looking.

Bottom-up LRIC is a constructivist methodology for determining forward-looking service cost. The methodology involves simulating the cost incurred by an efficiently operated network, using best available technology, to provide the service. Bottom-up LRIC models are highly recommended for regulatory decisions, though highly criticized for their lack of realism. The LRIC methodology takes into account fixed costs caused by the provision of interconnection services, but does not take into account the common costs, which do not vary proportionally with the provision of interconnection services. In practice, the implementation of LRIC models requires a systematic assessment of demand and cost evolutions, as well as the interdependencies that may result. A systematic analysis of network element load factors is also critical to accurately size the resources needed to convey the incremental traffic. In other words, the LRIC methodology makes

---

▌ Box 3.1 | Different Definitions Selected for Cross-Subsidization[10]

- **The public policy view**: From a public policy perspective, cross-subsidization occurs in a regulated industry when the regulated firm uses revenues from one market to keep operations in another market that is financially not viable. The cross-subsidy is considered anticompetitive if there are cash flows from noncompetitive to competitive markets. The cross-subsidy is considered a universal service obligation (USO) if the cash flow (1) goes anticlockwise; (2) occurs only because regulatory rules create it; and (3) would not occur if the government policy were absent, and/if the markets were competitive.

- **The cost allocation view**: In more general usage, if a service's prices do not make a reasonable contribution to overhead costs, it could be argued that the service is not carrying a fair share of the overheads, and is, therefore, being subsidized.

- **The Baumol-Faulhaber view**: Baumol and Faulhaber have taken the view that cross-subsidization occurs when prices for a service do not cover the service's incremental cost and the company still earns a normal profit (that is, zero economic profit) overall. This implies a maximum price of stand-alone cost.

- **A more comprehensive economic view**: More recent economic studies have shown that cross-subsidization occurs when prices for a service are higher than would be charged by the next most efficient competitor, and the company still earns a normal profit.

it possible to base the cost determination on forward-looking costs and not on historical costs. The next section provides a more extensive description of the LRIC methodology.

The LRIC Concept

The LRIC methodology, also sometimes referred to as the long run average incremental costs (LRAIC) methodology, estimates additional costs incurred in producing a service, relative to the costs already incurred by producing a portfolio of other services. The incremental costs of a service or element A somehow represent the cost savings, which result from not producing or not implementing A. In other words, the costs incurred to produce A over and above the portfolio of existing products are considered as the incremental cost.

The long-run concept involves taking the costs incurred in a long-term perspective. In the long run, production fixed costs can be considered as being variable costs. The long-run incremental costs of a service or element A therefore represent all of the costs that could be avoided if A were not produced or implemented. Hence, the incremental costs include all the costs directly attributable to A, whether these are variable in stricto sensu (depending on the level of traffic at a given capacity) or fixed (making up the capacity).

However, A can also make use of elements, services, or functions needed jointly with other services or elements. **The incremental costs** (even long run, strictly speaking) **only take into account a portion of these costs in the case of joint costs** (pro rata their incidence), **and not common costs.**[11] Incremental costs are important in the sense that they reflect the company's decision for producing A. Usually, in deciding to produce A, the firm expects that revenues generated by A should exceed the incremental cost incurred and provide an earning income to capital above the cost of capital.

Nonetheless, incremental costs, as we have just strictly defined, are difficult to use in pricing access to a service or network element, to the extent that they only cover part of the costs. Given that A also uses other network's resources and is partly responsible for joint costs incurred by the firm, it is necessary to allocate to A a portion of these joint costs. By adding all

these costs to the generic LRIC, we obtain a total service (TS) or total element (TE) LRIC. TSLRIC or TELRIC involves allocating **pertinent**[12] **joint and common costs** to A.

Finally, it is worth outlining how the cost allocation is implemented in practice. Two options are generally considered, although either of them can also lead to an alternative:

1. Historical costs form a first option. The method therefore involves evaluating the costs on the basis of their accounting values,[13] possibly adjusted to take inflation into account.
2. The forward-looking or current costs are the costs that would be incurred if the production system were rebuilt on the date of calculation.

The first approach is often described as a top-down approach and the second as a bottom-up approach. This is even more essential if we introduce a consideration of technical progress in cost evaluation. In fact, the production of A on the date t by an incumbent may not require specific new investment, but will result from investments already made in previous production cycles. As a result, working with outdated technology (the network architecture unchanged) or with a better architecture, as available on date t, are options that can be considered. In retaining the historical production system, we end up using historical costs or current costs to value the incremental cost of producing A. Conversely, in retaining the most efficient current production system, we end up valuing the incremental cost of producing A with current costs. For practical reasons, an "average historical" architecture[14] is generally selected. This point will be discussed in more detail later.

We then assume that:
1. The operator is an efficient operator that minimizes costs for a given production volume.
2. The costs are current costs.

As we have seen, this accounting and historical method involves breaking down the company's costs and allocating them among its different products. While assigning directly attributable costs to respective products is a straightforward issue, allocating joint and common costs is complex and sensitive. *The difference between* *the FDC and the TSLRIC method, using historic accounting costs and technologies, therefore resides in the nonincorporation of **nonrelevant common costs**.* Beginning with a total cost estimate obtained with an FDC approach, we can move to LRIC, step by step, by removing layers of cost inefficiencies as shown in figure 3.2.

Effective regulation of interconnection costs, therefore, introduces the following concepts: the specific nature of costs and the pertinence of costs.

The increment generally relates to a group of services using the same production infrastructure. The costs incurred from the provision of a specific service of the family should be determined within that framework. For example, a telephone company supplies retail and wholesale services. The cost incurred from providing retail services should be derived from the incremental costs incurred from providing wholesale and retail telephony services. However, the costs for marketing retail telephone services are costs that apply

to retail services and are not shared with the interconnection services. Inversely, interconnection services generate specific costs, which should not be included in the increment costs (for example, co-location costs for new entrant's equipment, costs for links between the incumbent's network and new entrants' networks, cost of modifying the information technology [IT] systems, specific billing cost, interconnection management service cost, and so forth). These costs should be passed on to interconnection customers only. To enable the provider to recover the costs incurred, a two-part tariff scheme is usually applied.

The concept of pertinence affects the handling of joint and common costs. Joint and common costs can only be applied to the increment on the condition that they are linked to it, either directly or indirectly. Revealing a causal link takes for granted that an in-depth technical review of the cost structure is performed. Common costs include research and

Figure 3.2 | Transition from Historical Accounting Costs to Economic Costs (LRIC)

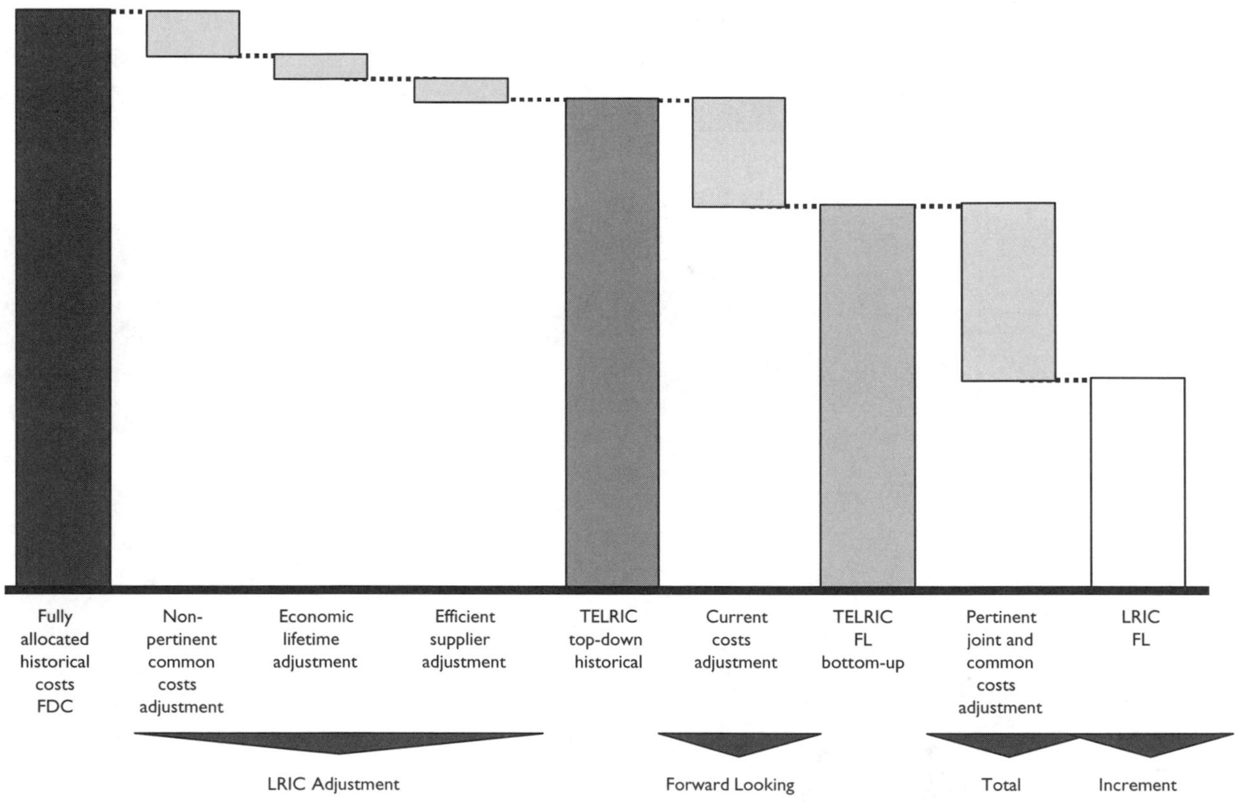

| Fully allocated historical costs FDC | Non-pertinent common costs adjustment | Economic lifetime adjustment | Efficient supplier adjustment | TELRIC top-down historical | Current costs adjustment | TELRIC FL bottom-up | Pertinent joint and common costs adjustment | LRIC FL |

LRIC Adjustment   Forward Looking   Total   Increment

Note: FL, forward looking.

development costs, costs associated with headquarters expenses and the operator's operational structure, costs for staff members who are no longer in their positions or are on leave, costs related to developing the brand name reputation or marketing, and costs associated with unused buildings. Among these costs, the regulator has to assess and decide which ones are pertinent to be accounted for. Only pertinent common costs can be allocated proportionally to interconnection services. Figure 3.3 illustrates the distinction between these different categories of costs.

In general, there is a risk in overestimating common fixed costs. For instance, the former monopoly could argue high common costs to "squeeze" out its competitors in downstream retail markets by reporting to interconnection some of the costs derived from competitive activities. In consequence, it is necessary to ensure that the common costs attributed to the increment are sound. In any case, the costs attributed should reflect the costs borne by the most efficient operators.

In practice, a certain number of questions are raised in regard to the theoretical framework discussed. These questions are synthesized in the two points below:

- Depending on the network services or elements considered, the TELRIC method can prove to be less favorable to new entrants than the FDC method. If a network section A is subject to substantial depreciation, and if current costs for reconstructing A are quite similar, or even higher than the historical costs, a TELRIC can lead to a higher cost

than the one that could be derived with an FDC assessment![15]

- Depending on assumptions made, the TELRIC method can lead to a relatively wide range of estimates. It is important to recall that directly attributable costs result from the service or elements segmentation assumed in the model. Therefore, the magnitude of joint and common pertinent costs depends on the segmentation refinement. Furthermore, allocating joint and common costs remains a major hurdle, even though the use of more accurate distribution criteria can induce smaller cross-subsidization between services or products.

Selecting specific TELRIC methods leads to some kind of arbitrage exercise, which is similar to positioning of a cost cursor within bounded values. The cost value (obviously high), which is supposed to be favorable to incumbents, will be at one extreme; at the other extreme will be the cost value (obviously low) that favors new entrants. Two other considerations are advanced in regard to positioning this cost cursor:

- "Theoretical" considerations limit the admissible spread of cost values, by suggesting that the spread be constrained by the implementation of a system eliminating cross-subsidization, and that resulting estimates be below the separate cost of providing the same services.

- "Political" considerations related to the appropriate economic signal are provided to market players and enable them to arbitrate between investing and purchasing the inputs from the incumbent (for example, the play or pay principle). Two concerns are, however, raised. The first concern is to ensure that input prices are not below the costs incurred by the incumbent. The second concern is to ensure that input prices allow for efficient allocation of resources.

An excessively low rate for input can lead to cross-subsidization toward this service and send undesirable signals to the market. An interconnection price below cost (in case of an efficient operator) could also endanger alternative infrastructure development, as that should make new investments less attractive and profitable. Conversely, an interconnection price above cost (in case of an efficient operator) is also likely to bias the market by switching demand to infrastructures that are

Figure 3.3 | Cost Structure

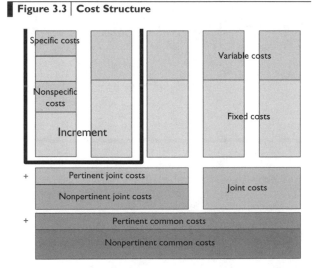

actually less efficient, and does not enhance productive efficiency in the sector. More specifically, the incumbent does not have the incentive to shift to a more efficient production process.

It is, therefore, up to the regulator, using cost models to determine the "correct" price level for this input. In so doing, the regulator collects and handles various information and has to fix a certain number of the model's parameters. These parameters and assumptions are improved on, with use and time.

Unfortunately, regulators and operators do not have a good knowledge of the industry cost structure. Therefore, the TELRIC bottom-up method represents a decision-making tool that induces improvements on procedures and processes implemented by regulators or operators to collect and retrieve cost information. This also improves the quality of investment decisions for firms, as it naturally enhances the transparency of the interconnection services market.

The following section reviews questions raised by the LRIC method for determining interconnection cost. The model deals with the issue of economic pricing of interconnection services and does not cover issues related to co-location or management services that are associated with interconnection.

Advantages and Drawbacks of LRIC

The following subsection summarizes the main advantages and drawbacks of the LRIC methodology. With these comments in mind, we expect the user to be able to outline the limitations of the LRIC methodology and notice how its implementation can help in sorting out and, probably, in clarifying a complex and sensitive subject.

One of the most effective features attached to LRIC pricing schemes is the sharing of the productivity gains that the various market players could derive. In so doing, implementing LRIC pricing schemes impedes excessive profits by the interconnection service provider. The relevance of the LRIC methodology therefore depends on the efficiency concept. In so doing, interconnection rates are derived from a benchmark provided by an efficient operator. Cost models are, indeed, developed to simulate, with some accuracy, the cost frontier that could prevail in a specific economic and market environment. Interconnection rates

must, therefore, be equal to long-run incremental costs in order to maximize economic efficiency. LRIC pricing schemes are forward looking and provide better incentive for static cost efficiency. In a dynamic framework, the impact of LRIC methodology in determining interconnection rates remains inconclusive (Laffont and Tirole 2001).

Tight access pricing regulation prevents the incumbent, controlling essential facilities, from extracting all the monopoly rents related to its dominant position over these resources. Although these regulations encourage the efficient utilization of the resources, they can also discourage further investments, subsequently causing significant social welfare losses. This is the most probable risk that could be implied by ineffective access pricing regulation.

The LRIC methodology has been criticized by several authors. Salinger (1998) and Laffont and Tirole (2001) argued that LRIC regulation provides the regulators with a key tool to manage industry entry. It is, therefore, crucial to ensure that, whenever a mistake is made, it is made in favor of overinvestment rather than underinvestment.

In a long-run framework, firms can reassign their inputs according to input price and output. Whenever an output is unprofitable, firms can freely dispose corresponding assets by selling them or by dispatching them to other activities. However, in the telecommunications industry, most assets cannot be freely disposed, because exiting an activity is costly. As shown by Hausmann (1996), when the regulatory framework allows entrants to exit and divest some of their assets, and does not provide similar options to the incumbent, entrants are less likely to invest in building their own infrastructure.

Furthermore, the value of most telecommunications operators' assets with current available technologies is lower than their corresponding book value. Consequently, entrants have no incentive to build their own networks and will prefer using the incumbent's infrastructure. LRIC can, thus, introduce inappropriate incentives for entry, because of probable cross-subsidization from the incumbents to entrants.[16]

It is also worth pointing out that the determination of long-run incremental costs remains after all discretionary. Salinger (1998) suggests that the use of LRIC is theoretically sound, but its implementation in practice is rather complex and could undermine the profitability of the incumbent's investment if poorly executed. Similarly, Valleti (2001) argues that access charges based purely on LRIC are an appropriate benchmark when retail-level distortions are eliminated or dealt with effectively by other regulatory instruments. Consequently, when the incumbent's retail prices are not cost oriented because of universal service obligations or delays in rebalancing retail rates, there is a need to add a uniform markup to the LRIC estimates, although doing that does not reflect any sound economic analysis.

Another problem is related to the pertinence of the essential facilities concept in the telecommunications industry. Celani, Petrecolla, and Ruzzier (2002) pointed out the following problems that are not properly addressed. What telecommunications market segments could qualify as essential facilities? What assets can be considered as being essential facilities? This calls for a sound methodology that enables disaggregation of the access market segment in order to identify those eligible for the essential facility concept. Obligations could then be limited to these market segments.

In developing countries, the key market players are mostly multinationals. Regulators should therefore closely monitor how transfer pricing schemes are implemented between affiliates and mother companies. Similarly, an appropriate database on cost information should be developed to limit the scope of opportunistic behaviors.

Definition of Interconnection Services

Interconnection services are offered to operators (fixed-line or mobile network operators) in order to collect or terminate their traffic from or to other competing operators. In general, four major categories of traffic are distinguished, as illustrated below:

Origin–Destination	
Recipient of Interconnection	Supplier of Interconnection
Traffic collection	Traffic origination/termination
Traffic termination	Traffic origination

Traditionally, three possibilities are considered in regard to the network's nodes that handle the traffic collection or termination:

- When the interconnection is handled at a local switch, the service is termed local.
- When the interconnection is handled at a transit switch, with the latter serving only a limited or specified transit area, the service is termed single transit.
- When the interconnection is handled at a transit switch, with the latter serving or providing access to the overall network's nodes, the service is termed double transit.

In principle, whenever a network's topology and architecture are compared, the collection and termination costs are identical. The equality is not sound, but is established in principle. In fact, the lack of reliable data on possible routing alternatives does not allow for further distinction of the cost of handling a terminating or a collected call.

In other words, five interconnection services are generally considered:

	Origin–Destination	
Interface Point	Correspondent	Network
Local switch	Local	
Transit switch in the area	Single transit	
Transit switch in a different area	Double transit	Domestic transit
International switch		International transit

Domestic transit is generally calculated as the difference between double transit and single transit. International transit is a surcharge applicable to international calls.

The following diagram shows the entry points, depending on the nature of the interconnection service. International service as assumed in the model is routed via an international transit switch providing an entry point in the transit area covered. If the entry point is located in a different area, the cost of domestic transit has to be added.

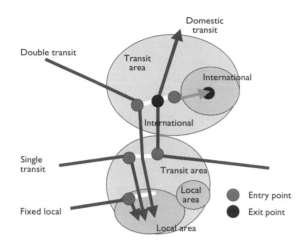

Figure 3.4 | Entry Points of Interconnection Service

Definition of the Increment

A telecommunications operator generally offers a wide range of services, whether to its subscribers or to other operators. These services have been traditionally classified according to their commercial nature. For instance, one usually differentiates local from long distance and from international services. Added-value services are also differentiated from plain old telephony services. However, another service classification approach is based on the use of network elements further described below. In general, there are three major categories of network elements:

- Elements that are dedicated to end users (which are used solely by a subscriber). These elements are generally found in the local loop network or access network and include a subscriber's connection line to the switch;

- Elements that are shared among users (dedicated to users on a dynamic basis upon request). These network elements are allocated temporarily to a subscriber and are generally found in the core telephony network.

- Elements that are shared by users but are used for the provision of complementary or supplementary services (telephone card services or other services offered by intelligent network features).

The three services discussed above can be labeled as: (a) access services, for services dedicated to each user, (b) transport services, for services shared among a network's users and offered by the core network func-

tions, and (c) value-added services, for shared services offered by intelligent functions of the network. Transport services can be broken down in various elementary services, according to traffic collection and delivery points. A correlation can be established between these elementary services, and the services marketed by the operator. Such a correlation is illustrated in the table below:

Table 3.1 | Correlation Matrix between Retail Services and Elementary Services

	Subscription Connection	Local Communication	Long Distance Communication	Supplementary Service	Interconnection Service
Retail sales service	X	X	X	X	
Added-value service				X	
Transport service					
Local		X	X		X
Single transit			X		X
Double transit			X		X
Access service	X	X			

As shown in the matrix, there is a correlation between the operator's elementary services (represented by horizontal lines in the first column) and services sold to end users (represented by columns in the first line). The matrix provides, for each service, the cost components incurred for its provision. Of course, the matrix is not exhaustive. A column representing leased lines could also be added to it. For instance, the provision of interconnection services involves transport services (local, simple, double transit). Conversely, the provision of a local communication involves in addition to transport services, the retail sale service.

Furthermore, an operator may wish to implement a retail pricing strategy that is not necessarily cost oriented, at least, as an entry strategy to develop its business line. In such situations, the operator will likely opt for a pricing strategy featuring high connection fees and low rental charges. Sector regulation should preserve the pricing freedom as long as it does not introduce a squeeze and distort competition (that is, as long as it does not eliminate new entrants from the market). It is therefore important to define and ensure the consistency between the pricing of the inputs needed to provide retail services and the pricing of the retail services. The table below provides an illustration of the linkages to help process the consistency review.

The retail sales activity includes all the functions associated with providing the service and managing the customer relationship. The retail sales activity purchases all the horizontal services required to provide the final service that the end user consumes. In so doing, it implicitly transforms respective cost elements used into pricing components. In checking the cost structure of regulated services, *the regulator must pay specific attention to the squeeze that could materialize as a result of undue cross-subsidization of competitively provided services by noncompetitively provided ones*. The regulator should also ensure that interconnection services, which are wholesale services, are priced below corresponding retail services.

As discussed earlier, the incremental cost methodology distinguishes directly attributable from nonattributable costs. It involves ascertaining, whether or not the production cost of "horizontal" service is increased, whenever a "vertical" service is added to the basket of other services produced.

Considering the example of interconnection services, it is important to underscore the following three conclusions:

- The provision of interconnection services does not modify the retail sales service, as the latter only concerns sales to final subscribers.
- The provision of interconnection services does not modify the access service, as the capacity implemented and its maintenance do not have to be adjusted to bear the flow of this additional traffic.
- In contrast, transport services are affected by the traffic resulting from interconnection services.

As a result, the cost of access services must be covered by retail service revenues. Unless these services rates are rebalanced, there are risks for anticompetitive practices and cream skimming. In other words, market deregulation imposes a certain cost orientation for dominant operators' tariffs, and, consequently, implies a price restructuring that eliminates the largest existing pricing averaging.[17]

The core network is used to provide a broad range of services. Apart from interconnection services, it facilitates the provision of retail services, including the provision of other services such as leased lines. Leased lines are either aimed at final customers (companies for their corporate networks), or at other telecommunications that operators can use to roll their own networks. The operator can also use leased lines for its own internal consumption (to operate another network such as the telex network, packet data transmission network, or even in many countries to carry the radio and television programs).

It is also important to note that the core network usually shares resources with other networks managed by the operator, or with the access network whose ducts are frequently shared in urban areas. It is important to report to the core network portions of the joint costs incurred by other networks and, in particular, the access network.

In conclusion, the increment to be considered for the calculation of interconnection service costs comprises the core network and excludes the access network's elements that are dedicated to users.

Table 3.2 | Matrix of Inputs Needed to Provide Retail Services

	Retail Sales	Subscription Connection	Local Communication	Long Distance Communication	Supplementary Service	Interconnection Service
Retail sales activity		X	X	X	X	
Added-value service	X					
Transport service						
Local	X					X
Single transit	X					X
Double transit	X					X
Access service	X					

Application to African Telecommunications Networks

African telecommunications networks are specific because of their early development stage. Excluding South Africa, we can define a representative African country (Afriland) with respect to its telecommunications common specificities. To do that, we aggregated data for a sample of 40 countries and were able to derive relevant common features, which are embodied in this cost model.[18]

The Average Size of an African Telecommunications Network

Afriland, as an African representative country, is characterized as follows:

Table 3.3	Snapshot of Telecommunications Development in Africa in 1999

Situation in 1999	Low Income, Low Teledensity Africa (40 countries)	European Union (15 countries)	Afriland	Average EU Country	Ratio
Area	20,927,000 km²	3,191,000 km²	525,000 km²	215,600 km²	0.41
Population	600 million	376 million	15 million	25 million	1.67
Population Density (inhabitants/km²)	29	117	29	117	4
GDP/capita	300 €	21,000 €	300 €	21,000 €	70
Total GDP (billions of euros)	180	7,900	4.5	525	117
Stock of main lines	3,140,000	200,000,000	75,000	13,300,000	180
Teledensity (fixed)	0.5%	53.2%	0.5%	53.2%	100
Density of lines/km²	0.15	61.8	0.14	61.8	440

Source: BIPE 2001.

In terms of size, Afriland is larger though less populated than an average European country. Afriland is double the size of an average European country. Its population density is four times less, implying higher rollout and maintenance costs for telecommunications infrastructure than in densely populated countries. Furthermore, its average income per capita is 70 times lower than in EU countries, and the fixed teledensity is 100 times lower. The average consumption of telephone services is estimated at slightly more than 20 minutes per inhabitant per year. On average, only 20 percent to 25 percent of the population has access to a telephone within walking distance.

In terms of infrastructure, the coverage of the fixed-line network remains rather limited and connects about 75,000 lines. The number of subscribers connected to the mobile networks exceeds the subscriber base of the fixed network and is approaching 100,000. The mobile segment is served by two or three operators offering essentially prepaid services (95 percent of the consumers of mobile are prepaid).

Furthermore, approximately 80 percent of the stock of subscribers and 80 percent of the traffic is concentrated in the capital city. On the whole, the outreach of the network is limited to the most important urban centers. Extending the coverage to rural communities remains a major challenge for the years to come, as rural areas are also those with the lowest income and population density. As a matter of fact, 80 percent of the stock of telephones serves only 20 percent of the population. Consequently, if the teledensity is about 2 percent in the main urban centers of Afriland, it is only about 0.125 percent in the rest of the country, though the overall national teledensity is 0.5 percent. Afriland is characterized by a very low level of telephone service demand, which is a direct consequence of the limited income per capita.

The implications in terms of network architecture, topology, and costs are:

- The transit network is almost nonexistent. Usually, the transit functions are implemented in local exchanges or switches and are located principally in the capital and in two or three main cities.

- The transmission network has an unusual topology. When SDH rings are set up, they are used to connect telephone switches and their RCUs within the same urban center or region.

- The networks still reflect choices of technology made in the 1990s. The number of small digital switches operated is higher than what could be achieved by using modern technology. With the best technology available today, most of these networks could be equipped with only a couple (one or two) of digital switches. The scope of inefficiencies resulting from this technology legacy is rather great.
- To reach remote rural areas, subscriber concentration systems (TDMAs) are installed. These systems serve from 8 to 256 subscribers and use time division multiplexing technology, known as TDMA. TDMA cost per line is particularly high.[19]
- Fiber-optic systems are not yet massively rolled out. In many cases, the demand does not justify the rollout of broadband transmission systems; however, more and more operators are beginning to replace their microwave transmission links with fiber-optic cables.
- Finally, in some countries, domestic satellite networks are operated as a means of extending the coverage to isolated areas (rain forest, islands, desert).

The proposed model seeks to account for all these specific features so that the cost calculation can be as close as possible to the reality from which should be derived the industry cost frontier. As an illustration, TDMA systems have been included in the increment, though one could argue against inclusion. We have assumed, however, that telephony circuits implemented through these systems are not dedicated to a user, but are shared among all users of the network, including those connected to the RCU. As a result, we consider that the traffic generated by servicing the interconnection demand (termination, origination) contributes to the sizing of these systems.

Nevertheless, in costing the interconnection service, the model provides two options:
- A cost "with TDMA systems" included in the increment.
- A cost "without TDMA systems" included in the increment.

The results obtained when including TDMA are very different from the ones obtained when it is not included. We suggest that the regulator decides, based on national specificity and according to the govern-

ment's universal access policy, whether or not to include the cost related to TDMA systems.

Nodes and Links

A thorough description of the core network is needed before its modeling is attempted. This description involves determining the types of nodes and the nature of the links between the nodes. In telecommunications, a node is generally characterized by a switching function, while the links form the transmission network. In developing the proposed cost model, we have assumed that an average African network has five types of nodes and five types of links.

These nodes are:
- Subscriber RCUs, which do not have independent switching command capacity, except in the event of a breakdown of the connection link with the host exchange. In the model, the small rural exchanges that are still in service and electromechanical exchanges have been considered as RCUs. The rationale is that digital RCUs are more likely to replace these old technologies.
- LSs to which RCUs are connected. Some of these exchanges have a transit capacity.
- "Pure" transit switches (TSWs),[20] which are rare in the African context, but are integrated into the model for the sake of completeness.
- ISs or international transit exchange. These exchanges are rarely taken into account in the modeling carried out in industrial countries because the international transit node is not differentiated from national transit[21]. This is not yet the case in Africa where the international segment is not yet unbundled from the incumbent's monopoly.
- Finally, TDMA systems lead to two types of nodes:
  - CSs, which are generally coupled with associated switches to manage the signaling and the interface with the transmission systems component;
  - TSs, which are the base stations installed in rural communities to provide the last mile connection to subscribers.

Similarly, there are five types of transmission links:
- RCU-LS links are the transmission links between RCUs and their host exchange.
- LS-LS links are the transmission links between two different LSs. In some cases, these links could also

involve LS links to TSs, to the extent that the transit function is implemented.

- Specific links between transit centers (TS-TS).
- Links to ISs (between LS and IS). In certain cases, the IS function can also be implemented in an LS.
- Internal links within TDMA systems, or the links between the central stations and terminal stations.

As a result, we obtain the matrix representation provided below:

Table 3.4 | Matrix of Transmission Links

Nodes	IS	TSW	LS	RCU	CS	TS
IS						
TSW	To IS	TSW-TSW	TSW-LS			
LS			LS-LS	RCU-LS	(Local link)	
RCU						
CS						CS-TS
TS						

It should be noted that local links (LS-CS, RCU, and the central station in a TDMA system) are not often taken into account because of the frequent co-location of these nodes.

Transit

Because of the small size of African networks, local exchanges (LSs) generally provide transit function. Whenever the network becomes larger in size, in terms of coverage, local areas are generally grouped into transit areas. The single transit feature involves collecting or delivering traffic in the transit area. Conversely, double transit involves collecting and terminating traffic beyond the initiating transit area. When a network does not have a transit switch, the distinction between local and single transit becomes irrelevant.

For the purpose of the exercise conducted here, we will assume the hierarchy between interconnection services (intra-LS, single transit, and double transit) is established along the incumbent's local rates zones or derived from the administrative or government territorial organization (municipalities, counties, districts, provinces, regions).

The first option links the interconnection services hierarchy to the retail pricing structure of the incumbent, while the second option, although more arbitrary, does not.

Notes

1. General interest obligations can be imposed, for example, access to emergency numbers.

2. Article 13 of the draft "Directive on a Common Regulatory Framework for Electronic Communications Networks and Services." 2001. Com 380, European Commission.

3. This measure supposes a prior definition of the relevant market, that is, the one in which power has to be measured. In general it is a market that brings together products among which significant substitutions and complementarities are present or possible from the customer point of view.

4. Definition from the draft "Directive on Access to Electronic Communications Networks and Associated Installations, as well as Their Interconnection." 2001. Com 369, European Commission.

5. The regulator can impose an obligation on a vertically integrated company to make its internal wholesale and transfer prices transparent in cases where the market analysis reveals that the operator concerned supplies facilities that are essential to other service providers, whereas it is itself in competition with these in the same market downstream ("Directive on Access to Electronic Communications Networks and Associated Installations, as well as Their Interconnection." 2001. Com 369, European Commission).

6. "Directive on Access to Electronic Communications Networks and Associated Installations, as well as Their Interconnection." 2001. Com 369, European Commission.

7. Strict economic definition.

8. For example, notions of opportunity cost. (In our context, a cost that enables the party selling the resource to a third-party "wholesaler" to obtain remuneration equivalent to that which it would have obtained by selling it in the end market. This cost is therefore the sale price less the cost of the retail price. It is equivalent for the supplier to sell on the intermediary market or on the final market. In some ways, it is an access cost for resellers.)

9. This is assumed to be undertaken here in year 1 (otherwise, it would be necessary to take the discounted sequence of investment costs).

10. Mark A. Jamison, available at http://bear.cba.ufl.edu/centers/purc/primary/jamison/Pricing.pdf.

11. Joint costs refer to costs incurred by two or several products in the same production process, in a constant proportion. We talk of common costs when the costs are incurred by several products and remain unchanged regardless of the relative proportion of these products (the salaries for operators' headquarters functions), that is, when a product is offered, the second product is produced by the same production without a supplementary cost.

12. That is, which demonstrate a causality relationship.

13. These are also referred to as embedded costs.

14. By taking over the topology of the historical network, that is, the same interconnection equipment locations inside the network (switching, concentration, distribution and so forth). This is, thus, the scorched node option, which involves retaining the net-

work's real hierarchy and the current traffic management rules. Imagining an optimum network would lead to a certain number of criticisms concerning its feasibility, and its possible operational capacity, on the impact of this virtual architecture on other prices.

15. This explains that in several countries, the FDC method was considered as the most favorable to new entrants in terms of access to the local loop, where civil engineering costs are dominant, although less favorable in terms of interconnection.

16. LRIC discriminates between incumbents and entrants in favor of the latter.

When incumbents make investment decisions, technology that the regulator may consider to be best may not be available.

17. Within this context, for operators who have not undertaken the required price restructuring for whatever reason, there may be a continued need to subsidize some loss-making services from profitable services and, on an almost general basis, a subsidy from international and long distance calls, to the access and/or local communication service. In this case, two phenomena have to be distinguished: the interconnection service must measure the value of these cost-oriented services and a possible temporary "access deficit" (until the price restructuring is achieved) must compensate for the pricing equalization in force.

18. This roughly means African countries whose gross domestic product (GDP) per inhabitant is lower than EUR 1,000.

19. These radio concentrators are presented in appendix 3.

20. Also called a tandem switch.

21. This has to do with market liberalization, which has now enabled operators to establish interconnection point of presence across the borders.

4 Modeling Principles

The model reconstructs a network, as would be done by an efficient operator using a forward-looking LRIC methodology. The reconstruction of the network is done in line with the realities of the Sub-Saharan African environment, as discussed earlier. Before discussing the modeling in detail, let us recall the following principles.

The Modeling Principles

A Long-Run Approach

The LRIC method adopts a long-run approach. The reconstruction of all network elements is assumed at year 1 and includes the increment.

A Forward-Looking Approach

Selecting a forward-looking approach means considering both the best technologies available and their current costs. From a pragmatic viewpoint, this comes down to considering the digital technologies available on the shelves today. Consequently, when modeling, we replace old technology with modern "equivalent" technology, which is more efficient and cost-effective.

For the transmission system, forward looking implies selecting SDH systems over fiber-optic cables. Although fiber optic is considered to be the most flexible, efficient, and economic technology in regard to the bandwidth unit cost, it is not yet rolled out systematically in Africa.

As regards the costs to be taken into account, these have to be estimated at the current acquisition price, and not at book value. As such, the decision whether to invest or purchase services (pay or play) should be made in the light of the prevailing economic situation.

An Efficient Approach

The cost modeling must reflect decisions made by an efficient operator, producing the increment services at the best cost while taking into account the technologies available. As a result, the model simulates a network that, at a given production level, minimizes the total cost by using best available technologies.

This requirement raises a certain number of questions with respect to the network architecture. As we have already stated, an incumbent inherits a network topology, which is largely determined by successive generations of technologies. Therefore, in dealing with the efficiency problem, there are two possible approaches:

- Modeling a network providing the expected services after optimizing its topology and architecture and eliminating the technology legacy. This option is called "scorched earth."
- Keeping the existing network's topology (the location of network nodes), while reconstructing the nodes and links with the best available technologies. The result is, in a way, a topologically identical network. This option is called "scorched node." It is the one selected in the proposed cost model.

If the resulting topology is clearly nonoptimal as it would be recommended to ensure production efficiency, then the regulator can prescribe a better network configuration.

Beyond the choice of the best technologies with an existing network structure, the question of efficiency as regards network operation also arises. Digital technologies, in general, and, more precisely, current network monitoring and management systems, make it possible to downsize factors of production, buildings space, labor, and so forth. Regulators and operators must agree on the optimum level of efficiency. LRIC models should not, under any circumstance, take into account excess staffing from previous management because market deregulation should be a strong incentive for the incumbent to improve its efficiency.

An Economic Approach, Not an Accounting Approach

To obtain cost annuity, it is necessary to transform the long-run incremental costs incurred, including those resulting from investments, into an annuity. An accounting approach would have led to considering yearly depreciation installments based on accounting lifetime of respective equipment, calculated according to fiscal criteria (linear, tapering, or accelerated depreciation). The cost annuity is determined here using an economic approach. Economic-oriented costs are assumed to be the effective tool for regulating industry entry and investments. It is assumed that entry or investment decisions are made on the grounds of profits or reasonable return on investment expected from the activity. In the proposed cost model, investment costs are converted into annual economic costs, as described in appendix 1.

To proceed further with the discussion, we now need to introduce the cost of capital concept. As described in appendix 2, the cost of capital represents the cost incurred by sponsors or promoters in mobilizing financial resources. The cost of capital concept factors in technology progress, economic, and country-specific risks.

A Bottom-Up Approach

Two main alternative approaches can be used to estimate the long-run average incremental costs: the top-down model and the bottom-up model. These two approaches can be summarized as follows:

* Top-down cost models rely on the accounting data and allocate costs to different services on the basis of the causality correlation between the costs and

services. In some cases, top-down models are also implemented with current costs.
* Bottom-up cost models imply the development of engineering and economic models in order to calculate the costs of network elements used to provide particular services, assuming an efficient operator that uses best available technologies.

In principle, both methods should lead to the same result. In fact, this can only happen if the same assumptions are made for operation efficiency and depreciation. The proposed cost model belongs to the second category.

The Working Units

The model has to determine unit interconnection costs. It is, therefore, necessary to select a metric system. Traditionally, the traffic flow through the core network is measured in minutes. The cumulated duration of calls, measured in minutes, is considered to be the important parameter in determining costs. However, some interconnection prices and some cost models also take into account the number of calls.

In practice, network elements also handle the following noninvoiced traffic: (a) the call set-up time, (b) the closing time, and (c) the time spent in handling unsuccessful calls. The sizing of some network elements therefore depends on the number of calls conveyed. This is particularly relevant for switching elements that have to handle call attempts.[1] The number of calls essentially continues to determine the cost incurred by the temporal occupation of noninvoiced network elements (waiting time and unanswered calls). The cost per minute is, by convention, the representative unit cost.

The Model Structure

The logical structure of the model is relatively simple:

* The model begins by proposing a nomenclature of network elements (nodes and links).
* Each service uses these elements in different proportions. On the basis of routing factors, the model calculates the total load supported in traffic minutes for each element.
* The model sizes network elements specifically for the transmission system, within the confines of the topology the user chooses.

- The model then aggregates network elements costs.
- The model finally calculates the interconnection costs, depending on what network elements are used to supply the service.

The network is made of network elements. Any communication or any interconnection service (which is a special form of communication) uses, on average, x times each of these elements (with x varying from 0 to a few units at a maximum). The x factors are called routing factors. This allows for the calculation of the traffic flow per network element. The model calculates the investment cost incurred to satisfy the traffic demand and derives respective operating costs.

	Investment costs	Operating costs
Attributable costs		
Common costs		

The operating costs consist of two terms:
- A cost subcomponent, proportional to investment costs and reflecting the cost of maintenance and direct operation of network element (spare parts, equipment section of preventive and corrective maintenance, energy consumed).
- A cost subcomponent for the staff allocated to operations.

For small and spread-out networks, the staff cost can hardly be evaluated as a percentage of investment costs. For the sake of accuracy, the user is requested to state a reasonable number of staff required to run the network. The model then uses unit labor cost input to calculate the total of operating costs and divide it among the number of network elements.

Obviously, investment costs are subject to detailed calculations. Based on an estimate of the volume of traffic to be handled by each network element, and the unit cost for each element, the model determines the total investment cost. To achieve this, the amount of traffic assigned to each network element at peak time is used for its sizing. Using the unit investment cost per network element, the model calculates the total investment cost per element. The operating costs are allocated to the investment unit costs to obtain a global cost per element. A unit cost per minute handled is then obtained by dividing the global total by the total volume of traffic handled. These costs per minute are then added up to reflect the network elements involved in handling a specific interconnection service request. They are then adjusted by the hourly gradient applied to retail services to obtain the final interconnection rate.

To sum up, the model reconstructs the costs of the network at two levels:
- At the level of nodes (switching elements), investment costs are structured in fixed and variable components according to BHE (business hour Erlangs transformed into 2 Mbps) and to the number of subscribers, respectively.
- At the level of links, calculations are done at two sublevels:
  - A transmission level at which electronic transmission equipment (mainly on SDH rings) is designed and sized;
  - An infrastructure level at which the link substratum is designed. Generally, the infrastructures comprise three types of technologies: trenches, microwaves, and satellite links.

The trenches are broken down by geo-type (urban, suburban, and rural) corresponding to different burying techniques (wrapped trenches, ducted, buried). The microwaves are characterized by the nature of their masts (light, medium, or heavy).

The links are sized by the traffic at peak times expressed in capacity (Mbps) and are sized to handle the switched telephone network traffic, as well as leased lines bandwidth. Assumptions regarding the sharing of certain elements of basic infrastructure with other networks (for example, access networks) subsequently allow for the sharing of costs, which are not fully borne by the core network.

To sum up, the model computation modules are provided in the following 21 sheets structured as follows:
- A menu sheet for the user navigation.
- Twelve sheets forming the core piece of the model described afterwards.
- Four sheets specific to mobile networks (whose results appear on the general results sheet).
- One sheet on the sensitivity of the model to some parameters.
- Three specific management sheets (two sheets for the publication of fixed and mobile reports and a

sheet to manage the two languages and the default values).

The 12 sheets in the general model break down as follows:

- Four sheets to gather the assumptions.
- One sheet to calculate the traffic and sizing of the network elements.
- Two other sheets to size the transmission and infrastructures.
- Three sheets to calculate costs (switching, transmission, and infrastructures).
- One sheet to recapitulate the total costs (including the common costs) and to calculate the unit costs per minute and element.
- One sheet to present results.

The core of the model is synthesized in the following diagram:

Figure 4.1 | Cost Model Architecture

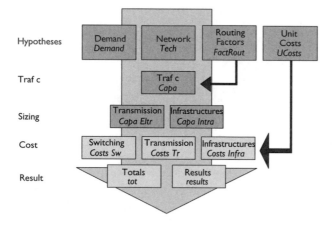

Applications of the Cost Model

In practice, the cost modeling exercise enables regulators and operators to improve their knowledge of the industry cost structure and its efficiency frontier. Of course, the challenge is managing the information asymmetry that characterizes the regulator and the regulated firm relationships. The following are the three main advantages that cost models can provide:

- Providing a catalytic effect on cost information collection and retrieval by both the regulator and the regulated firm. To run the model, the regulator draws up a comprehensive list of required informa-

tion from the operators and sets up procedures for the ratification of the information supplied (for example, by means of accounting audits, establishing ABC, reviewing investment invoices).

- Focusing the benchmarking on a limited amount of sensitive information used as inputs for the decision process. As a result, the regulator shifts away from standard benchmarking of tariffs observed between countries to benchmarking key input or parameters.

- Providing the opportunity to the regulator to improve on its information and knowledge about network architecture and topology. With a better understanding of the network structure, the regulator can refine procedures implemented to collect information from regulated operators. In fact, data collection must be executed according to formal and recurrent procedures.

In conclusion, it is important that regulators ensure the confidentiality of the information collected from operators. Despite most national regulations that give regulators inquiry powers, additional attention is needed to ensure and preserve the confidentiality of the collected information. In general, newly established regulators do not yet have sound and effective safeguard measures ensuring the confidentiality of information collected from operators. Unless such measures are implemented, it is likely that regulated operators will remain reluctant to fully disclose their strategic information.

Like other costing methodologies, LRIC models also have consequential limitations, which are related to the wide scope of assumptions that foster their development. A system of check and control handled in collaboration with the industry can limit the arbitrariness of the most sensitive assumptions. The following are likely to be among the most sensitive model parameters that should be reviewed:

- The selected network topology (number and location of nodes).
- The percentage of traffic at peak hour and other demand data critical to sizing the network elements.
- The traffic growth as predicted by the industry.
- An estimate of the staff number that could be considered "efficient."

- Major cost drivers specific to the country and how they impact the investment costs in comparison with international best practice.
- The proportion of joint and common costs.
- The problematic decision to factor in TDMA concentrator systems in the increment leading to the calculation of interconnection cost.

A contradictory discussion on the model assumptions would most likely improve on the accuracy of the range of cost estimates provided. This accuracy will improve as procedures prevailing to data collection also improve. It will also improve the soundness of the argument against the theoretical criticism of LRIC models.

Note

1. As a matter of fact, for a long time the number of call attempts during peak time (business hour call attempts [BHCA]) was used to specify the overall processing capacity of switching exchanges. In view of the enhanced processing power of available processors and the resulting decreasing cost of memory, the number of calls processed at busy hours is no longer a relevant criterion to effectively differentiate switching systems. Vendors now agree to consider the total duration of calls (measured in Erlangs) and the number of subscribers accessing the node as the most important engineering parameters for switching exchange design.

5 User Guide

The cost model includes a friendly interface. It was developed as a Microsoft 2000 Excel file that contains several folders. The model depends on several macro commands written in Visual Basic. In other words, the program cost model is less than 1 mega-octet in size; hence, it is easily portable.

After launching the program, the user can choose whether or not to activate the macros links. Activating the macros is essential for the Menu sheet functions.

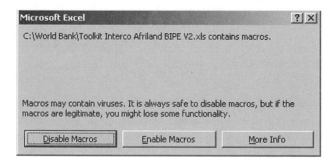

After the macros are activated, the user is asked to select the language. There are two options: French or English. The model is then presented with captions in the selected language.

Once the language is selected, the Command/Menu sheet is shown:

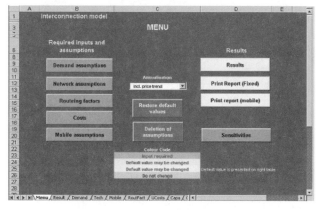

This sheet includes three sets of commands:
- On the left is a column allowing access to the Assumptions menu.
- In the center is a column providing access to the Options menu.
- On the right is a column allowing the user to display or print out results and test their sensitivity.

IMPORTANT: Save your working file in a different name.

Filling in the Assumptions

The assumptions are entered on five sheets, which are accessible via the Menu buttons in the left column of the Menu sheet:

- Demand assumptions.
- Network assumptions.
- Routing factors.
- Cost elements assumptions.
- Specific assumptions for the mobile network.

The color code used to differentiate cells is as follows:

- Blue cells: exogenous assumptions to be filled in by the user. These assumptions characterize the network and are essential for the modeling.
- Light green cells: default information that can be modified. These assumptions can be shared by different networks.
- Light blue cells: default values that can be modified. These default values are computed by the user and are, generally, presented in a table on the right. However, to run the model with provided default values, the user should avoid modifying the filled matrix that contains default routing factors.
- Dark green cells: result cells, which under no circumstances should be changed.

It is not advisable to attempt modification of the model program or Visual Basic macros, unless one has a good knowledge of computer programming. The entire range of sheets and all the formulas are accessible. The user can follow a step-by-step overview of the model's computation process. However, modification[1] outside the sheets that are accessible via the Menu sheet (and the dark green boxes on these sheets) may alter the model's performance.

Demand Assumptions

The Demand sheet is accessed via the Demand assumptions button on the menu (see below).

Traffic Data

The incumbent's traffic has to be broken down into 11 traffic categories. The total traffic in minutes has to be placed in the first column. In the second column, the average call duration in minutes (with at least 1 or 2 decimals) is provided by type of calls. The total number of calls is then calculated in the third column. Finally, the predicted growth rate applied to the traffic volume (in minutes) that is used to measure the network is entered in the fourth column.

The traffic growth rate should remain moderate, to avoid major oversizing of the network. The cost calcu-

Existing traffic over incumbent's network	Number of minutes	Average length of calls	Margin for growth (%) Number of successful calls	Number of minutes
Local telephony			0	
Internet calls			0	
Long distance			0	
International				
* incoming			0	
* outgoing			0	
Calls to mobiles				
* domestic			0	
Calls from mobiles				
* domestic			0	
* international			0	
Interconnection				
* local			0	
* long distance			0	
Others (Kiosk, switched X25 etc.)			0	
Total	0		0	

lation is done on a yearly basis. As a result, the model considers the predicted increment of the traffic for the year under review.

The following input is needed for the calculation:

Traffic statistic	Successful calls	Unsuccessful calls
Average call set-up time in seconds (time to answer)	15	30
Percentage of successful calls	75%	
Traffic in busiest hour of the year (as a percentage of the total)	0.00040	

First of all, the average answering time for successful and unsuccessful calls is taken by default at 15 and 30 seconds. The percentage of successful calls is taken at 75 percent. These values can be modified.

The percentage of the total traffic at the peak hour (business hour) is used to size the network's capacity. This value is estimated by default at 0.04 percent (= 0.00040), but can be modified. It is considered that there are 335 peak days in a year (11/12 of the year), with on average 7.5 peak hours per day. This gives in all 2,513 peak hours per year. The total peak hours only represents 1/2513 of the total annual traffic, hence 0.04 percent. The user should note that this variable is extremely sensitive and exerts a direct impact on the sizing of the network.

The "gradient," which is related to retail services pricing schemes, should be calculated. The model proposes five pricing levels: a peak rate, a reduced rate for off-peak hours, a reduced rate for weekend rate, and two other reduced rates to fit with more refined pricing schemes, if needed.

In the first column, the breakdown of the total traffic is entered as a percentage for each pricing level discussed above. In the second column, the level for each pricing level is entered in relative terms, with the peak hour rate being the reference. For example, if the peak hour rate is 60 cents and the reduced rate is 40 cents, we will enter 40/60 = 0.667 in the second box of the second column of the table.

The gradient is calculated in column 3 and will be used to calculate interconnection rates in these different pricing ranges.

Retail rate gradient (ratio)	Traffic (%)	Rates 100 = peak	Gradient
Peak		100	
Off-peak			
Weekend			
Other 1			
Other 2			
Average		0	

Subscribers

Data on subscribers and their connection mode are requested in the second part of this sheet. First, the network topology is filled as follows:

Node information	RCU	LS	TSW	IS	CS	TS	Total
Number of nodes (total)							0
Nodes linked by satellite							0
Other nodes not linked through a SDH ring							0
Nodes on SDH rings	0	0	0	0			0

The first line of this table contains the total number of nodes in each category. We will count:

- RCUs: the total number of remote concentrator units included in the network.
- LSs: the total number of local exchanges equipped with their own processing and command units. LSs may also perform domestic or international transit functions.
- TSWs: transit exchanges, dedicated exclusively to handling domestic transit.
- ISs: international exchanges, dedicated to international transit.
- CSs: central stations for TDMA systems, used to extend the network coverage to rural communities.[2]
- TSs: terminal stations in TDMA systems, used to connect about 40 subscribers.

The second line of the table deducts the nodes accounted for in the first line, and which are connected through the domestic satellite system. In general, only RCUs or LSs are connected by satellite. The other nodes of the network are assumed to be connected to each other through SDH rings. However, these rings are not always rolled out for several reasons. The third line of the table deducts the nodes already accounted for, and which are not connected by SDH rings. This represents an arbitrage in terms of efficiency that regulators should assess and decide upon. These nodes will be connected by microwave, at a higher cost than that of equivalent SDH rings. The last line then calculates the number of nodes interconnected by SDH rings.

The following table shows data relating to the subscribers' connection:

Form of subscriber connection			
Percentage (%) of installed lines:	Installed capacity	o.w. TDMA systems	
– Remote Concentrator Units and rural switches			
– Local switches			
Total	0		
o.w. % on local switch with transit capabilities			
o.w. % on local switch without transit capabilities			
Percentage of subscriber lines connected to:	Used capacity	o.w. linked by satellite	o.w. non-linked by SDH	o.w. TDMA systems
– Remote Concentrator Units and rural switches				
– Local switches				
Total	0	0	0	

The first two lines should provide the installed **capacity** of the RCUs and LSs. This total appears on the following line, beside which the total capacity of the TDMA systems is indicated. The two following lines enable the user to enter the proportion of subscribers' lines connected to RCUs and LSs. It also allows for access to the proportion connected to LSs with transit features. Doing that improves the accuracy of the routing factor estimates.

The table also includes information on the **stock of subscribers** (connected capacity), and differentiates those connected to RCUs from those connected to LSs:

- The first column contains the total number of network subscribers.
- The second column contains those connected to nodes linked by satellite.
- The third column contains those connected to nodes that are neither linked by satellite or SDH rings.
- The fourth column contains the total number of subscribers connected by TDMA systems.

Leased lines	Number	Margin for growth (%)
Analogue leased lines (64 kbits/s equivalents)		
Digital leased lines (64 kbits/s equivalents)		
Number of local tariff zones		
Number of LS with transit capabilities		
Number of TS interconnected to mobile networks		
Ratio od traffic from TDMA subscriber to non TDMA subscriber		
Share of direct long distance calls between LS		
% of direct routes between LS with transit capabilities		

First of all, the user enters the number of 64 kbps equivalent analogue or digital leased lines. The user also provides the predicted growth rate to be taken into account for network sizing. It should be remembered that all the links using the core network must be taken into account:

- Telegraph and telex lines.
- Leased lines provided to private or public users (banks, transporters, civil service departments, police, army).
- Leased lines provided to third-party operators (mobile networks).
- Leased lines used by the operator to set up data transmission networks (X25, Frame Relay, IP networks).
- Leased lines eventually provided to carry TV and radio programs.

This is followed by additional information on refining the default calculation of the routing factors:

- Number of local pricing zones.
- Number of LSs with a transit function.
- Number of exchanges (LS-TS) where there is an interconnection with mobile networks.
- Ratio of the average traffic for a TDMA subscriber relative to a non-TDMA subscriber (generally lower than 1).
- Proportion of the long distance calls between LSs through direct routes.
- Proportion of direct routes between LSs with a transit function.

Main Technical Assumptions

This second ("Tech") sheet containing complementary assumptions concerning the network is accessed via the Network assumptions button on the menu. This sheet enables the user to enter important assumptions on the network structure.

Main Assumptions on Switching Exchanges

We start with a small number of assumptions whereby default values are proposed:

Co-location of switches				
Percentage of tandem switches co-located with local switches	50%			
Maximum number of nodes on a ring				
Maximum number of nodes on a ring	16			
Utilization level of switching nodes (%)	RCU	LS	TS	IS
Used capacity (Erlangs)	95%	95%	95%	80%

The first assumption relates to the percentage of transit switches co-located with LSs so that the host buildings are not counted twice. If the network does not include transit switches, the assumption is not used.

The second assumption refers to the maximum number of nodes connected by an SDH ring. The default value is 16 nodes.

Main Assumptions for Transmission Links

In transmission, a link is the media over which information is conveyed between nodes. The information is conveyed through different routes that may exist over transmission links connecting the nodes. The number of routes that can be created between nodes only depends on the network security constraints.

The first step is to determine the number of 2 Mbps channels that are needed to carry the traffic flow. Consequently, the user is asked to provide information characterizing the transmission routes.

	RCU-LS	LS-LS-TS	to IS	CS-TS
Utilization level of transmission elements (%)	60%	70%	80%	50%
Erlangs per circuit	0.5	0.6	0.7	0.6
Average length of transmission routes across all geo-types in meters				

- In the first line, the load of the transmission elements is provided as a proportion of the total capacity available.
- In the second line, information on traffic expressed in Erlangs is provided.

The information provided above is used to compute the size of the transmission network and the number of ports for each switching exchange.

The average length of transmission routes across all the geo-types is then filled. The average route length is the means of length routes between two nodes.

The following table portrays the transmission network structure for SDH systems. On the right, bandwidth capacity used for each link has to be provided.

	Distribution of traffic links		
Mix of STM systems in a fully SDH transmission network	RCU-LS	LS-LS-TS	to IS
STM 1			
STM 4			
STM 16			
STM 64			
Total = 100%	0%	0%	0%
Note: These may be re-allocated to meet required capacity.			

Box 5.1	Erlang

An Erlang is a telecommunications traffic measurement metric. For example, if a group of users makes 30 calls in 1 hour and each call has an average duration of 5 minutes, the total traffic flow is expressed as follows:

Minutes of traffic = number of calls x duration = 30 x 5 = 150
Traffic in Erlang = 150 / 60 = 2.5

Agner Krarup Erlang was born in Linborg, Denmark, in 1878. He was a pioneer of telephone traffic analysis. He proposed a formula for calculating the proportion of callers served by an exchange who are compelled to wait for their turn. In 1909, he published his first result, titled *The Theory of Probabilities and Telephone Conversations*. His work earned him worldwide recognition, as well as that of the British General Post Office, which endorsed his formula. He worked for 20 years at the Copenhagen Telephone Company until his death in 1929. During the 1940s, the Erlang became the accepted unit for measuring telephone traffic.

Routes are distributed according to their bandwidth needs. That makes it possible to size the electronic transmission elements. These indications can be adjusted to the maximum number of authorized nodes per route. These calculations are carried out in the Capa ElTr sheet.

The following are additional default values used in the computation of the network size:

Average length between microwave towers (meters)	40,000
Distance between regenerators (in meters)	64,000
Utilization level of leased lines	100%
Diversity for STM multiplex and LTES (percentage)	15%
Other equipment	
Transmission cross connects per IS	2
Diversity for regenerators	2
Number of repeater stations of TDMA systems	
Utilization level of satellite transponders (%)	

The first indicator shows the average distance between installed microwave towers (in meters). The default value is equal to 40 km. This length depends on the relief, stretches of water, and so forth.

The second indicator shows the average distance between regenerators on SDH rings. The default number is equal to 64 km. The load factor of leased lines is taken at 100 percent.

The diversity indicators make it possible to take into account the specificities of the real topology and their implications, with respect to an optimized topology retained by the model.

Main Assumptions on Infrastructures
This part of the Tech sheet captures all the assumptions needed to determine the size of the infrastructures.

The first table captures the total length of infrastructures per type of technology:

Length (meters)	RCU-LS	LS-LS-TS	to IS	Total
Total length of trench by transmission link (meters)				0
Total length of microwave by transmission link (SDH closure)				0
Total length of microwave by transmission link (non-SDH)				0
Total (meters)	0	0	0	

The model distinguishes the total length (in meters) by type of:
- Trenches.
- Microwave networks closing SDH rings.
- Microwave networks supporting non-SDH links.

The cost distribution between LS-LS-TS and TS-TS is provided:

	LS-LS	TS-TS
Breakdown of transmission and infrastructure costs between single and double transit	75%	25%

Trench specificities are provided: (a) wrapped trenches in urban environment, (b) ducts in suburban environment, (c) buried trenches in rural environment. The user is asked to fill in the distribution that is relevant:

Proportion of total length of trench in each geo-type (%):	RCU-LS	LS-LS-TS	to IS
– urban (duct)			
– suburban			
– rural (buried)			
	0%	0%	0%

Then, some complementary indicators related to the cable network are required:

Trench sharing	
Percentage of trenches that are shared by geo-type:	
- urban	
- suburban	
- rural	0%
Percentage of shared trench attributable to conveyance	25%
Cables	
Cables per duct	1

- The percentage of trenches (wrapped/ducts) equally shared with other networks, including the access network, the cable network, or a private transmission network. In general, fully buried cables are dedicated to a single type of network.
- The percentage of trenches not equally shared with other networks. In general, in such circumstances, the core network only occupies about 25 percent of the trench's capacity. This is given as a default value.
- The number of cables per duct (generally one).

This is followed by assumptions concerning microwaves.

Microwave			
Closure of SDH rings	RCU-LS	LS-LS-TSW	to IS
Number of routes			
Non-SDH routes	RCU-LS	LS-LS-TSW	to IS
Number of routes			
Breakdown per capacity			
34 Mbps			
8 Mbps			
2 Mbps			
	0%	0%	0%

How many SDH rings are closed by microwaves? Microwave links considered for closure operate at 155

Mbit/s. For non–SDH **routes,** the user is asked to fill in information on the number of routes per link type equipped with microwave, and the distribution over 34, 8, and 2 Mbit/s microwave.

Cost elements for microwave sites are discussed next:

% of shared masts on different routes				
Backbone network				
TDMA systems				
Percentage of microwave routes served by different masts:	RCU-LS	LS-LS-TS	to IS	CS-TS
– Light				
– Medium				
– Heavy				
Total	0%	0%	0%	0%

- How many routes share the same microwave sites? What is the distribution between the core and access networks, or the TDMA network?
- How many links share the same antennae masts?
  - Light mast (lower than 40 meters)
  - Medium mast (between 40 and 60 meters)
  - Heavy mast (higher than 60 meters)

Other costs shared between the core and the access networks are discussed:

Site costs	Access	Core	Other
Percentage of RCU sites attributed to service	50%	50%	0%
Percentage of LS sites attributed to service	50%	50%	0%
Percentage of TDMA TS sites attributed to service	30%	70%	0%
Percentage of site costs allocated to transmission (as opposed to switching)	25%		
Percentage of TDMA costs allocated to transmission (as opposed to switching)	15%		

The following costs are attributed to the core network by default:

- 50 percent of the costs for the RCU and LS site.
- 70 percent of the costs of the site for terminal stations in TDMA systems.

The following are attributed by default to the switching node:

- 25 percent of site costs (and therefore 75 percent to transmission).
- 15 percent of TDMA system costs (and therefore 85 percent to transmission).

Main Assumptions on Operation

Finally, this Tech sheet provides the number and the distribution of staff between the core network, access, and other activities.

The user is asked to provide an estimate of the number of staff considered optimal by an efficient operator. The total obtained is then distributed over the switching, transmission, and infrastructure activities:

Personnel (core network)	Number					
Switching						
Transmission						
Infrastructure						
Breakdown	RCU	LS	TS	IS	CS	TS
Switching	25%	25%	0%	5%	15%	30%
	RCU-LS	LS-LS-TS	to IS	CS-TS		
Transmission	15%	50%	5%	30%		
Infrastructure	15%	50%	5%	30%		

Main Assumptions on Routing Factors

The RoutFact sheet is accessed by the Routing factors button on the menu. This sheet includes 12 routing factor matrixes.

A table showing the default routing factors calculated on the basis of the information supplied in the two previous sheets is placed on the right. A similar blank table is presented on the left, allowing the user to enter his/her own computed routing factors if the default values calculated are unsuitable.

The first three tables are the routing factors for the fixed-line network, while the latter three are for the mobile network. In each case, the first two tables indicate how many times on average each type of call uses each network element. The first information is for the "nodes" elements and the second is for the "links" elements. The latter indicates how many times each type of interconnection service uses these same elements (nodes and links) on average.

IMPORTANT: As soon as a blank table is filled in by the user (even a single box), it will be taken into account by the model. Any table that substitutes for the default table must therefore be filled in completely. Some boxes can be left empty, but all of the boxes that do not have a null value must be filled in. The user can specify a table without having to specify them all.

The first table relates to the nodes:

Routing factors	RCU	LS	TS	IS	CS	TS
Local telephone						
Internet calls						
Long distance						
International						
— incoming						
— outgoing						
Calls to mobiles						
— domestic						
Calls from mobiles						
— domestic						
— international						
Interconnection						
— local						
— long distance						
Others (Kiosk, switches X25 etc.)						

Thus, the first line should indicate how many RCUs, LSs, and TSs are crossed on average by a local telephone call and, subsequently, for all the types of calls according to their characteristics.

The second table requires the same information for the different types of links, while adding leased lines:

Routing factors	RCU-LS	LS-LS-TS	to IS	CS-TS
Local				
Internet calls				
Long distance				
International				
— incoming				
— outgoing				
Calls to mobiles				
— domestic				
Calls from mobiles				
— domestic				
— international				
Interconnection				
— local				
— long distance				
Others (payphone, ISDN, etc.)				
Leased lines				

Finally, the third table gathers the same information for each interconnection service:

	Local level	Single transit	Double transit	Transit	International transit
Switching					
RCU					
LS					
TS					
IS					
CS					
TS					
Transmission					
RCU-LS					
LS-LS-TS					
TS-TS					
to IS					
CS-TS					

This third table covers both the nodes and links.

Main Cost Allocation Assumptions

The Ucosts sheet is accessed via the Costs button on the menu.

This sheet includes four major series of assumptions:

1. General assumptions on costs.
2. Assumptions in regard to common costs, and applying to attributable costs calculated by the model.
3. Assumptions in regard to the unit costs for each network element for the fixed-line network.
4. Complementary assumptions for the mobile network.

General Assumptions

These assumptions are important. First, they relate to the currency in which the results will be presented and the costs calculated. The name of this currency is sought in the first line and then its exchange rate to euros.

The model can be run with local currency or in euros or U.S. dollars. An exchange rate is provided for the conversion into local currency. The proposed cost model uses the euro as the reference currency, but this reference can be easily changed. Consequently, default unit costs are expressed in euros.

The model then requires three elements of supplementary information on the investment cost:

	Model currency	Local currency versus Euro	Euro
Name			
Exchange rate versus Euro			1,000
Customs and transit duties			
Market surcharge		Total	
Insurance and freight		100%	
	Model currency	Euro	Local currency
Annual cost of an employee			
Options for cost annuity:	1	1	annuity including price trend
		2	annuity without price trend

1. The first is the level of the customs and transit duty applied to imported telecommunications equipment. In general, customs duties can be very high, though, temporarily, exemptions are often granted to operators as part of incentive schemes implemented in order to develop foreign direct investment. In the proposed cost model, it is assumed that all imported equipment is subject to custom duties.

2. The second is a market surcharge reflecting price distortions related to the small size of African economies. This surcharge applies to imported equipment. Equipment prices in Africa are generally higher than international prices. Because of the tiny size of African telecommunications markets, orders placed by operators are small in volume. Consequently, African telecommunications operators' negotiation power, vis-à-vis major vendors, is limited.

3. The third is related to transport and insurance costs that are significantly higher for landlocked countries.

These extra charges considerably increase the cost of imported equipment. The model provides the opportunity to factor in this consideration when reviewing the network's costs. Salary and labor costs are in local currency. These costs are obtained by dividing the staff expenditure incurred by the operator by the number of employees.

Finally, the model requires that the user clearly show how cost annuities are computed. For further details on different methodologies, the reader is referred to appendix 1. Two options are provided: (a) option 1 is to factor in the equipment price trend in the computation; (b) option 2 does not integrate any price trend for the equipment. In general, the user will select an option that takes into account the price development of each network's element.

The following are the key elements of the financial calculations:

1. Appendix 2 reviews the cost of capital calculation. Information required to compute the cost of capital is provided below.
2. The user introduces the margin of working capital needed to efficiently operate the network. This is provided as a percentage of the total attributable and common over investment and operating costs.

Level of gearing [D/(D+E)]	35%
Risk free return	8%
Average rate of return of the overall market	15%
Risk premium on stock (beta coefficient)	0.80
Risk premium on debt (spread)	2%
Income tax rate	35%
Cost of capital (pre-tax) (%)	10.0%
Working capital surcharge (%)	0.0%

The cost of capital resulting from the assumptions described above is then presented in a dark green cell.

In other words, the operator offering interconnection services has two options to finance its investment: debt and equity. The gearing ratio captures the leverage exposure of the operator. Debt and equity are usually priced at different rates as their respective risks are dif-

ferent. Equity has a risk premium calculated on the basis of the average return on investment observed in the local stock market and a sector-specific factor (beta coefficient). Meanwhile, debt has a specific risk premium factor.

Common Cost Assumptions

The second part of the sheet deals with the common costs ratio. There is no strict standard in this area. The applicable common cost ratio does not necessarily have to be the ratio derived from the operator's books. The ratio should refer to those observed from efficient operators. This is an area for which the regulator should conduct effective benchmarking.

The following are the default values provided by the cost model:

Common costs attributed to in %	RCU	LS	TS	IS	CS	TS
Investments	5%	5%	5%	5%	5%	5%
Operation	10%	10%	10%	10%	10%	10%

Common costs attributed to in %	RCU-LS	LS-LS-TS	TS-TS	to IS	CS-TS
Investments	5%	5%	5%	5%	5%
Operation	10%	10%	10%	10%	10%

Common investment costs include, for example, the vehicle fleet, other investment at the headquarters, and so forth. These costs are distributed among the firm's activities.

Unit Cost Assumptions

The following unit cost assumptions are considered for each network element:

Equipment X	Equipment Price local currency	User input local currency FAB	Default value Equipment Price Euros FAB	Installation costs (% of capita costs)	Asset life (years)	Price trend (%)	Evolution of Capital* price	Scrap value as a % of equipment capital cost	Operating costs as a percentage of equipment capital cost (%)
Equipment X									
Fixed cost of equipment	—		147,000	10%	11	–8%	0.92	1%	3.0%
Cost per line	—		10	10%	12	–8%	0.92	1%	2.0%
Cost per trunk	—		1,500	10%	12	–8%	0.92	1%	2.0%

1. 1st column (column C in the model): contains the result of the unit cost calculation. The user should avoid changing this information. This value derives either from input placed in the third column (expressed in euros) or from the value entered by the user in the second column. The following calculation is done :

   a. On the basis of the default value expressed in euros (third column), the exchange rates and the three rates stipulated for imported equipment (customs, market surcharge, and transport) are applied;

   b. On the basis of a value entered by the user (entry in column 2, column D, and takes precedence over the default value) in local currency, and two of the three rates stipulated in reference to imported equipment (customs and transport, but no market surcharge) are applied.

2. 2nd column (D): data entered by the user as a unit cost that is more suitable than the default cost. Data in **national currency** takes precedence over the default cost.

3. 3rd column (E): default value of the unit cost expressed in euros.

4. 4th column (F): equipment installation cost (as a percentage of the capital cost). This cost includes possible engineering costs (survey, planning, design), costs for monitoring and possibly inspecting the manufacturing process, the installation costs per se, the costs for system testing, and costs for training (on site or abroad). This column contains a default value, which can be modified by the user.

5. 5th column (G): an economic lifetime and not an accounting lifetime. This duration is implicitly adjusted if cost annuity is done according to option 1 (price trend). This lifetime is determined by the equipment's operating longevity, availability of spare parts, and so forth. This column contains a default value that can be modified by the user.

6. 6th column (H): price development trend. This is the trend for the long-term development of equipment cost (+ or − x% per year). The column contains a default value that can be modified by the user.

7. 7th column (I): contains the cost of capital and of the price development. This value is used to compute cost annuity when option 1 is selected.

8. 8th column (J): residual value of the equipment at the end of its lifetime. The residual value is deducted from the capital cost used in calculating the constant economic annuity. It is primarily significant for buildings and sites for which the land keeps a high residual value. This column contains a default value that can be modified by the user.

9. 9th column (K): operating cost incurred by the equipment as a percentage of the capital cost. This cost is the operation-maintenance cost incurred directly by the equipment, and does not include staff or labor costs. It comprises spare parts, repair costs, and expenditure for equipment consumables (energy). This column contains a default value that can be modified by the user.

The number of unit cost items amounts to 68 and is grouped below as follows:

- Eighteen headings for switching.
- Twenty-four headings for transmission (SDH electronics, microwaves, towers).
- Nine headings for infrastructures (cables and ducts).
- Four items for other costs (including one related to mobile networks).
- Thirteen cost headings specific to mobile networks.

Some of the headings deserve the following specific comments:

- Locally supplied equipment or local construction (buildings, civil engineering) are not subject to imported expenses (custom duties and taxes).
- Cost heading related to Domsat repeaters; leased lines for mobile networks belong to operating cost.
- For some investment, the model does not identify specific cost items. These investments are assessed as a percentage of investment cost implied by a basket of items. The model selects four baskets for these complementary investments:
  - Switching investments: this item includes everything needed for the operation of basic services, excepting value-added services, and does not show price entered in the equipment. This applies to: SS7 signaling, signal transfer points (generally included with the switches), synchronization, centralized network management systems and, possibly, training equipment.
  - Transmission investments: this includes everything related to centralized management, alarm

checking, and testing and installation equipment that is not included in material supplies already accounted for.

- Infrastructure investments: testing, layout, installation equipment.
- Mobile investments: items equivalent to the mobile networks that are not included in the unit prices for equipment.

In general, the cost of network elements is divided into two categories of cost item:

1. The fixed cost of equipment (processing unit of a switch, racks, management bays). These costs vary with capacity (subscribers, BHE, number of fibers).
2. The cost of the site where the equipment is installed.

The site costs deserve clarification. In general, the site includes the following cost elements:

- Land acquisition cost.
- Land development and building costs (fencing, access road).
- Specific costs for fitting out buildings (technical floors, air conditioning, protection against lightning and fire, security system).
- Energy cost.
  A telecommunications building often contains:
- Switching and transmission equipment.
- Equipment for the core network or for the access network, and even for other activities (for example, accommodation for public telephone boxes, a sales branch).

Consequently, site costs should be shared out among the various activities. The model handles the allocation of these costs in the Tech sheet, which has already been reviewed. The cost for sites (like civil engineering work) is considered to be a locally provided service. Hence, it is not subject to the three rates specified in the model (customs, market cost overrun, transport). The same applies to costs of masts and microwave sites.

Assumptions for the Mobile Network

Several assumptions in the preceding sheets are used to calculate interconnection costs for mobile networks. This, in particular, is the case with the Cost sheet reviewed earlier. Nonetheless, specific demand and technical elements are required to determine mobile

network costs. These are entered in the Mobile sheet, which the user can access via the Mobile assumptions button on the Command (Menu) sheet.

The sheet is organized into three major sections:

1. Demand assumptions.
2. Subscriber and network assumptions.
3. Operating cost assumptions.

Demand Assumptions

The user can enter aggregate traffic elements carried by the mobile network, similarly to what was done for the fixed-line network:

			Margin for growth (%)	
Existing traffic over mobile network	Number of minutes	Average length of calls	Number of success-ful calls	Number of minutes
Outgoing				
Internal			0	
to mobile network			0	
to fixed network			0	
Incoming				
from mobile network			0	
from fixed network			0	
Other (CRM…)				
Other (CRM…)			0	
Total	0		0	

Demand and network elements for mobile are, of course, different:

	MSC	BSC	BTS
% of internal calls using the same…	80%	60%	20%
Traffic Statistics	Successful calls	Unsuccess-ful calls	
Average call set-up time in seconds (time to answer)	15	30	
Percentage of successful calls	77%		
Traffic in busiest hour of the year (as a percentage of the total)	0.0005		
Retail tariff gradient (ratio)	Traffic (%)	Tariffs 100 = peak	Gradient
Peak		100	
off-peak			
Weekend			
other 1			
other 2			
Average		0	

In addition, the model indicates the proportion of internal calls that terminate in the same mobile switching center (MSC), base station controller (BSC), and base terminal station (BTS) area.

Assumptions for the Mobile Network
This section contains information that specifically characterizes the mobile network and is required for cost determination:

1. Capacity installed on MSCs and the number of subscribers:

	Number
Installed capacity (MSC)	
Subscribers (post-paid)	
Subscribers (prepaid)	

2. Equipment utilization levels:

Utilization level of switching nodes (%)	MSC	BSC-BTS	
Used capacity Erlangs	95%	80%	
	MSC-MSC	MSC-BSC	BSC-BTS
Utilization level of transmission elements (%)	90%	70%	60%
Erlangs per circuit	0.5	0.6	0.5

3. Node information:

Node information	MSC	BSC	BTS
Number of nodes (total)			
BSC co-located with MSC			

4. Data on BTSs:

BTS data	Total	per BTS	
Number of communications per TRX			4 < x < 8
Total number of TRX (Full duplex channel)			6 < x < 16
Number of sectors (cells)			1 < x < 6
Number of sites			< 1

The average number of calls transmitted by transmitter/receiver (TRX; this is the radio equipment that manages transmission at base station level) is between four and eight. The number of TRXs per base stations, and the number of sectors by the BTSs and the number of BTSs, are computed and entered by the user. These values are divided on the right by the number of BTSs to ensure that the average values obtained are actually within the technical ranges accepted.

5. Data on the transmission network of the mobile operator are entered when these links can be leased from the incumbent fixed-line operators or from any other licensed operator or are rolled out by the mobile operator (owned microwave or fiber-optic links).

Transmission network				
Microwave	MSC-MSC	MSC-BSC	BSC-BTS		Total
Number of routes				0
Total length (m)				0
Breakdown per capacity		Break-down of total routes		Break-down of total length
155 Mbps				
34 Mbps				
8 Mbps				
2 Mbps				

The user enters the type of link, the number of routes, length of routes, and distribution by capacity.

6. The breakdown of the number of masts is entered, thus:

Transmission electronics	MSC-MSC	MSC-BSC	BSC-BTS	MSC-MSC	MSC-BSC	BSC-BTS
155 Mbps				0	0	0
34 Mbps				0	0	0
8 Mbps				0	0	0
2 Mbps				0	0	0
			0			0
Total number of masts						
Percentage of different masts:						
– on roof						
– Light						
– Medium						
– Heavy						

The sizing of electronics equipment per link is done automatically. If the breakdown appearing in cells F76:H79 (model) does not match the actual situation, the user can enter the relevant data in cells C76:E79. The total number of physical masts should be entered in cell C81.

The model then requests a breakdown of masts in the following categories: (a) masts installed on roofs, (b) masts requiring light masts (<40 meters), (c) medium-sized masts (between 40 and 60 meters), and (d) heavy masts (>60 meters).

7. Leased lines used by the mobile network:

Leased lines (2 Mbps equiv.)	MSC-MSC	MSC-BSC	BSC-BTS
Urban – Number			
Nonurban – Number			
– Total length (km)			

The model requires differentiating urban and nonurban leased lines. The user is requested to enter the number of leased lines per type and per length.

Assumptions on Operating Costs

The Mobile sheet includes data needed to calculate the labor costs and their breakdown:

Personnel (network operation)	Number		
Switching			
Transmission			
Breakdown	MSC	BSC	BTS
Switching	25%	25%	50%
	MSC-MSC	MSC-BSC	BSC-BTS
Transmission	5%	15%	80%

The second part of the Cost sheet includes the assumptions required for common costs allocation. Data provided by default can be modified by the user.

Common costs attributed to in %	MSC	BSC	BTS
Investments	5%	5%	5%
Operation	10%	10%	10%
Common costs attributed to in %	MSC-MSC	MSC-BSC	BSC-BTS
Investments	5%	5%	5%
Operation	10%	10%	10%

The Results Sheets

After entering all the inputs and assumptions, the user can display, print, or test the sensitivity of the model's results. These buttons activate four sheets:

1. A Results sheet is displayed.
2. The user can print the model's results by selecting the fixed-line or the mobile network simulation. Each report includes the results and assumptions. However, the intermediary computations are not printed, though these can be displayed in different spreadsheets.
3. The user can test the results' sensitivity to predetermined parameter variations.

The Results

The simulation results for fixed-line and mobile operator are presented in Print sheets. Each simulation includes:

• Costs per minute for each network element.
• Interconnection services costs obtained from network elements costs as follows: network elements costs that are respectively multiplied by corresponding routing factors to derive interconnection service costs.

For the fixed-line network, the cost model provides the option to add rural TDMA systems costs to the interconnection service costs. The model provides two interconnection cost estimates. The first estimate includes TDMA systems costs, while the second one does not. Depending on universal access policies, the regulator will decide whether to account for TDMA systems costs.

	Cost per minute
Switching	
RCU	
LS	
TS	
IS	
CS	
TS	
Transmission	
RCU-LS	
LS-LS-TS	
TS-TS	
to IS	
CS-TS	

0	Local level	Single transit	Double transit	Transit	Transit international
Interconnection rates (with TDMA systems)					
Interconnection rates (without TDMA systems)					
Africa "Best current practice" peak rates (Model Currency)					
Europe "Best current practice" peak rates (Model Currency)					

Euros cents	Local level	Single transit	Double transit	Transit	Transit international
Interconnection rates (with TDMA systems)					
Africa "Best current practice" peak rates					
Europe "Best current practic" peak rates (Euros cents)	0.5 – 0.9	0.8 – 1.5	1.5 – 1.8	0.3 – 0.7	

The costs are expressed in the currency selected in the unit cost sheet. They are converted into euros for comparison purposes. *These costs are average costs.* They are then converted into costs according to time–of–day slots with the gradients specified in the demand assumptions:

For the mobile networks, the results provide the cost per minute for network elements and the cost of interconnection services. A distinction is made between call termination and origination, whenever justified by the routing factors.

Time of day charging (Model currency)					
With TDMA systems	Local level	Single transit	Double transit	Transit	Transit inter-national
Peak					
Off-peak					
Weekend					
Other 1					
Other 2					

Switching	Cost per minute
MSC	
BSC-BTS	
BTS	
Transmission	
MSC-MSC	
MSC-BSC	
BSC-BTS	

0	Originating	Terminating
Interconnection rates		
Euro cents		
Interconnection rates		

Time of day charging (Model currency)	Originating	Terminating
Peak		
Off-peak		
Weekend		
Other 1		
Other 2		

Printing Reports

Printing can be launched from the Menu sheet:

- Results and assumptions for the fixed-line network.
- Results and assumptions for the mobile network.

When launching the printer, the user is asked to provide a name for the printed simulation. When provided, the name is stated at the top of the printed report for identification purposes. The statement is not compulsory.

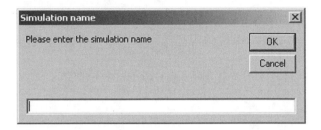

The document is printed using a print preview function that enables the user to change the format and adapt it to the available printer, if necessary. Printing generally requires eight pages.

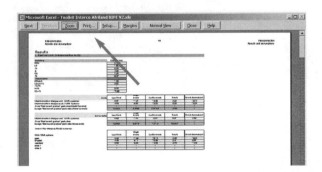

The printer selection box is called up by clicking on the Print button on the upper bar:

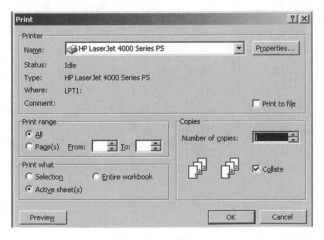

The printer and printing parameters can then be specified.

The same procedure applies to printing the mobile networks report.

Testing the Sensitivity of the Results

Once an initial determination of the interconnection costs is obtained, the sensitivity of the results can be tested. The user can perform the sensitivity analysis through the Sensitivities button on the Menu sheet.

A snapshot of the sheet is provided below:

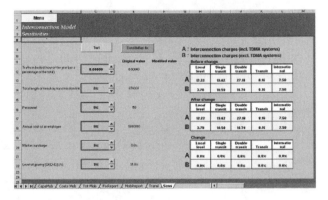

To test the model sensitivity, captions for six predetermined parameters are provided. The user can enter input as described below:

- Traffic at peak hours (as a percentage of the total traffic) (cell C31 of the Demand sheet).
- Total length of the trenches (sum of cells C48 to E48 of the Tech sheet).
- Total staff (sum of cells C105 to C107 in the Tech sheet).
- Average annual cost of an employee (cell E16 of the Ucosts sheet).
- Market surcharge ratio (cell C12 of the Ucosts sheet).
- Level of gearing [D/(D + E)] (cell C21 of the Ucosts sheet).

The user can modify these variables, either by entering a relative variation expressed in percentage (total length of trenches, staff, annual cost of an employee) or by adding to or subtracting from the original value, which is already a percentage (peak hour traffic, market surcharge, level of gearing).

The modification can be made directly by entering a value in the cell assigned for new value; the user can increase or decrease the variable value by utilizing the vertical "cursors."

The simulation is run by pressing the Test button when the new values are entered.

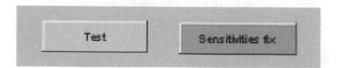

The original values and the new sensitivity parameter values appear in columns E and F of an Excel sheet. The new results can be compared with the old ones, as shown in the following table:

A :	Interconnection rates					
B :	Interconnection rates with TDMA cross-subsidization					
	Before change					
	Local level	Single transit	Double transit	Transit	International transit	
A						Old values
B						
	After change					
	Local level	Single transit	Double transit	Transit	International transit	
A						New values
B						
	Change					
	Local level	Single transit	Double transit	Transit	International transit	
A						Differences
B						

The user can iterate several sensitivity tests before confirming and saving the resulting values. This is done by pressing the Set sensitivities button, which opens a dialogue box that requests the user to either validate the modifications made or to cancel them.

If the user decides to keep original values, the model's assumptions are not modified. Conversely, if the user decides otherwise, the model's assumptions are modified accordingly. To be able to keep both original and new values, the user must save respective files in different names.

Managing the Model

- Users are advised to save completed simulations with suitable names. The user can clear the model's assumptions or restore the default values of the model.

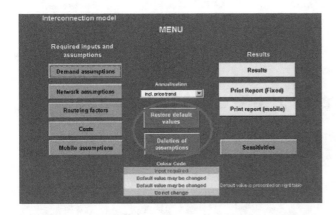

To run a simulation with the model, the user must:

1. Enter the different assumptions or parameters required. If needed, the user can also modify the default values provided.

2. After providing all the input, the user can display the results.

3. Test the sensitivity of these results to variations of main or key parameters.

4. Print out the reports, including the simulation results, along with the underlying assumptions.

IMPORTANT: Whenever a logical problem (such as division by zero) arises, or there is any inconsistency among assumptions, the model will not compute the interconnection costs. For example, sizing the capacity of SDH rings assumes that all input provided by the user is consistent with the traffic that will be conveyed. In this particular case, the user has to ratify the assumptions step by step. Doing this, he or she can either modify the capacity of the SDH systems (cells C26 to E31 of the Tech sheet), or review the calculations done by the Capa EITr sheet.

Notes

1. This includes the formulas as well as the layout (addition or suppression of lines or columns, and so forth).

2. Thus, a TDMA system connected to an exchange that included a capacity of 512 subscribers would count as two CSs.

6 Operations of the Cost Model

This section presents the proposed model in greater detail.

The model was developed using Excel 2000 and Visual Basic. All intermediary calculation sheets are in Excel 2000.

The model's synopsis structure is shown below:

Figure 6.1 | Cost Model Architecture

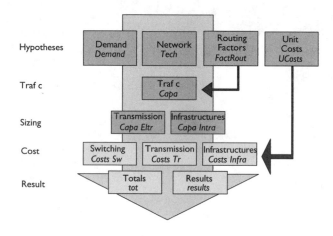

Assumption sheets are described in the user guide. This section further spells out how the intermediary computations are implemented by the model.

Basic Principles

The model builds on the breakdown of the core network, as discussed in previous chapters, into network elements. Eleven network elements are identified: six different types of nodes and five different types of links. These elements are extensively reviewed in chapter 2 of this guidebook.

In terms of sizing, LS-LS and TS-TS links are bundled under the same LS-LS-TS caption to take into account the fact that subscriber exchanges also offer transit features in Africa. As discussed in chapter 2, few African networks have dedicated transit exchanges. However, when calculating the interconnection costs, the model splits these costs into two categories: LS-LS links and TS-TS links.

To size the various elements, the model uses total and the peak hour traffic information. This is done by the Capa sheet. The network size is calculated for:

- Transmission electronics equipment (Capa ElTr sheet).
- Infrastructures (Capa Infra sheet).

After the sizing is done, the model calculates the network costs for each element:

- The nodes comprise the subject of a cost breakdown on the Costs Sw sheet.
- The link costs are broken down on two sheets:
  - The transmission costs are calculated on the Costs Tr sheet.
  - The infrastructure costs are calculated on the Costs Infra sheet.

Total traffic and costs (including the common costs) are consolidated before the model determines the unit costs (Tot sheet). The Result sheet then presents unit interconnection costs according to routing factors.

Logic of the Intermediary Spreadsheets

This section describes in detail the intermediary calculations.

Capacities (Capa Sheet)

This sheet calculates the total traffic and the peak hour traffic using the information on volume of traffic in minutes, as entered by the user:

a. The volume of traffic is adjusted to factor in non-billed traffic, which is costly (time needed to set up the successful calls. Column C: number of calls ★ average time to answer successful calls in seconds /60).

b. The resulting value is adjusted with the time consumed to convey unsuccessful calls (column D: column C + number of unsuccessful calls ★ average time to respond to unsuccessful calls/60).

c. This is then adjusted with the predicted traffic growth rate, as indicated in the Demand sheet.

d. As a result, the adjusted volume of traffic (invoiced and noninvoiced with a growth rate) is broken down by network element (four nodes and three links, excluding the radio concentrator equipping base stations of TDMA systems), based on routing factors provided in the RoutFact sheet.

e. The model provides the volume of traffic in minutes supported by each network element.

f. The total traffic obtained is converted into Erlangs (BHE) and used to size nodes and links. This information, depending on the charge factor of each element (percentage of occupation), is adjusted to ensure traffic fluidity.

g. In the case of links, these BHEs are transformed into Mbit/s.

h. The same calculation is applied to leased lines the number of which is converted into Mbit/s and adjusted with the predicted demand growth rate.

i. The core network's capacity is adjusted according to resources required by the public switched telephony network and leased lines traffic.

Transmission Capacities (Capa ElTr Sheet)

This sheet breaks down the transmission equipment, which includes add-drop multiplexers (ADMs) and termination equipment for SDH rings (STM 1, 4, 16, and 64).

a. The capacity of transmission elements is calculated.

b. An adjustment factor is then applied to oversize the capacity. The adjustment factor is taken equal to 1, by default. It can be adjusted in line 10, if exceptional factors that apply to certain types of links have to be taken into account.

c. The model then calculates the proportion of the link's capacity not handled by SDH links from subscriber connections, which are not connected to SDH links. In the case of international transit, the model assumes that links to the international transit exchange are point-to-point SDH. If this is not the case, the user should, herein, indicate the proportion of these links that do not use SDH technology (cell E11).

d. The capacity (in Mbit/s) that has to be served in SDH, in Domsat, and in non-SDH terrestrial lines is then derived (lines 12 to 14).

e. The model then considers the number of nodes and the positioning of the nodes with respect to links (lines 17 and 18), as well as the mix of SDH systems for the various categories of links (lines 27 to 30).

Three types of links are served by SDH technologies: RCU-LS links, LS-LS-TS links, and links to the IS. For each, the model calculates the number of rings needed. The algorithm builds on a former one developed by Europe Economics, and takes into account the maximum number of nodes per loop as entered in the Tech sheet (cell C10).

The simulation carried out assumes that RCUs are linked to LSs through SDH systems. LS-LS and LS-TS links are implemented through an upper-level SDH ring. The ring's capacity is sized according to the flow of traffic between its nodes. It is assumed that the minimal number of nodes to justify a ring is three. The traffic capacity that can be handled per ring is determined according to the following factors (STM 1, 4, 16, and 64):

- The number of rings constituting the core network.
- The average number of nodes per ring.
- The number of physical routes per ring (number of nodes + 1).
- The number of ADMs and termination multiplexers (MUXs) (2 ★ number of rings + total number of nodes).
- The number of regenerators.

Links to ISs are assumed to be SDH point to point and are, therefore, much easier to size. The following box summarizes the algorithm used by Europe Economics' model to size transmission links.

Infrastructure Capacities (Capa Infra Sheet)

This sheet sizes the infrastructures needed to roll out the core network transmission links. In general, there are two types of infrastructures:

- Trenches and ducts.
- Radio links.

The trenches are, themselves, differentiated in three subcategories, according to their location:
- Urban areas: wrapped ducts.
- Suburban areas: ducts.
- Rural areas: buried cables.

In the proposed model, aerial cables are not used for conveying traffic in the core network.

Box 6.1 | **Sizing of the SDH Network (example of RCU-LS routes)**

The transmission equipment required is evaluated by type of link.
- Capacity required in Mbit/s = total capacity required in Mbit/s (adjusted) taken in the assumption section of the same sheet.
- Distribution of the required capacity (Mbit/s).

STM1 = required capacity * total STM1 system mix (the two data items are taken in this sheet) (A)

STM4 = idem (B)

STM16 = idem (C)

STM64 = idem (D)

- Number of nodes = number of RCUs taken in the same sheet, assumptions section.
- Total number of nodes per STM1 capacity (STM1 share in the systems total by the number of nodes).

$$\frac{capacity\ required\ in\ STM(A)}{capacity\ required\ for\ all\ STM\left(\sum A - B - C - D\right)} * number\ of\ RCUs$$

- Same formula for the STM4, STM16. and STM64 systems.
- Same formula for the STM4, STM16. and STM64 systems.

STM1:

$$IF\left(\frac{number\ of\ nodes\ per\ capacity\ for\ STM1}{maximum\ number\ of\ nodes\ on\ a\ ring\ (\text{"technical" sheet})} \rangle \frac{capacity\ required\ for\ STM1}{maximum\ capacity\ of\ a\ piece\ of\ SDH\ equipment};\ then\ take\ the\ first\ term;\ else\ take\ the\ second.\right)$$

Column 2: the preceding result * by the maximum capacity of a piece of SDH equipment (same sheet in assumptions).
The same procedure is applied to STM4, STM16, and STM64 systems.
- Number of extra nodes needed to have at least 3 nodes per ring: logical function.

$$IF\left(\begin{array}{l} number\ of\ RCUs\langle 3 * \sum rings\ per\ capacity\ ;\ then\ marked\ \text{"check"};\\[6pt] else\ several\ cases\ are\ possible\ represented\ by\ logical\ functions:\\ IF\left(\begin{array}{l} 3 * (total\ number\ of\ STM1\ rings - total\ number\ of\ nodes(RCU)) \rangle\ 0;\\ then\ take\ this\ figure + IF(3 * the\ same\ thing\ for\ STM4);\ + IF(3 * \ the\ same\ thing\ for\ STM16);\\ + IF(3 * the\ same\ thing\ for\ STM64);\ else\ 0 \end{array}\right) \end{array}\right)$$

(Continued on page 55.)

| Box 6.1 | Sizing of the SDH Network (example of RCU-LS routes) (continued) |

- If we obtain "check" for the preceding calculation, i.e., if the number of RCUs is under 3 * the sum of the rings per capacity we then recalculate the total number of rings per STM1, STM4, STM16, and STM 64 capacity using an IF logical function.
- We recalculate the total number of nodes per capacity (STM1, STM4, STM16, and STM64) adjusted by 1 as a logical function again as a function of the calculation of the number of extra nodes needed to obtain at least 3 nodes per ring.

For example, for STM1 (the same formula is applied for the other capacities):

$$IF\left(\begin{array}{l}C39(cell-number)="check";\ then\ take\ a\ figure\ in\ the\ recalculated\ previous\ table\ i.e.,\\ number\ of\ nodes\ *\ number\ of\ STM1\ rings\ /\ total\ number\ of\ rings\ of\ all\ capacities;\\ \qquad\qquad\qquad\quad\left(\begin{array}{l}3*total\ number\ of\ rings\ per\ capacity\rangle\ total\ number\ of\ nodes\ (RCU)\ ;\\ else\ take\ a\ logical\ function\ IF\ \Big|\ then\ take\ 3*\ the\ total\ number\ of\ rings\ per\ capacity;\ else\ take\ the\ total\ number\ of\ nodes\end{array}\right)\end{array}\right)$$

- Reallocation of nodes on rings by capacity.

Column 1: for example for STM1 systems (the same formula is applied for other capacities):

$$IF\left(\begin{array}{l}C39="check";\ then\ take\ the\ number\ of\ nodes\ above;\\ else\ IF\big((number\ of\ nodes\ -\ 3*number\ of\ rings)\rangle\ 0;\ then\ take\ this\ number\ ;\ else\ take\ 0\big)\end{array}\right)$$

Column 2:

$$IF\left(\begin{array}{l}C39="check";\ then\ take\ 0;\\ else\ take\ (column1\ STM1/\sum column\ 1)*\ the\ number\ of\ extra\ nodes\ needed\ to\ obtain\ 3\ nodes\ per\ ring\end{array}\right)$$

- The total number of nodes by adjusted capacity 2:

For example, for STM1 (the same formula is applied for other capacities):

$$IF\left(\begin{array}{l}C39="check";\ then\ take\ the\ adjusted\ rounded\ number\ of\ nodes\ 1;\ else\\ IF\left(\begin{array}{l}the\ adjusted\ number\ of\ nodes\ 1\ =\ total\ number\ of\ rings,\ take\ the\ rounded\ total\ adjusted\ number\ of\ nodes\ 1,\\ else\ take\ the\ total\ adjusted\ number\ of\ nodes\ 1-\ preceding\ reallocated\ nodes\ column\ 2\end{array}\right)\end{array}\right)$$

- The average number of nodes per ring.

For example, for STM1 (the same formula is applied for STM4, STM16, and STM64):

$$SI\left(\begin{array}{l}C39="check";\ then\ IF\left(\begin{array}{l}total\ adjusted\ number\ of\ nodes\ by\ capacity\ 2\ =\ 0\ then\ 0\ ;\\ else\ \dfrac{the\ total\ adjusted\ number\ of\ nodes\ by\ capacity\ 2}{adjusted\ total\ number\ of\ rings}\end{array}\right);\\ else\ IF\left(total\ number\ of\ nodes\ by\ adjusted\ capacity\ 2=0;\ then\ 0;\ else\ \dfrac{adjusted\ total\ number\ of\ nodes\ by\ capacity\ 2}{total\ number\ of\ rings}\right)\end{array}\right)$$

- Average number of physical routes per STM1 =

    IF(average number of nodes per ring = 0; then 0; else take the average number of nodes per ring +1)

- Average number of physical routes per STM4 ring = same formula as STM1.
- Average number of physical routes per STM16 ring = same formula as STM1.
- Average number of physical routes per STM64 ring = same formula as STM1.

(Continued on page 56.)

| Box 6.1 | Sizing of the SDH Network (example of RCU-LS routes) (continued) |

- Total number of physical routes:

$$IF \left(\begin{array}{l} C39 = \textit{"check"}; \text{ then sommeprod (average number of physical routes } * \text{ total number of rings by adjusted capacity for b98} \\ = \textit{"check"}; \text{ else sommeprod (average number of routes } * \text{ total number of rings by capacity)} \end{array} \right)$$

The "sommeprod" function gives the sum of products of corresponding elements for several matrices :
sommeprod(matrix1;matrix2;matrix3;...)

- Number of termination systems = total number of physical routes (above) *2.
- Number of multiplexers (Gateway MUX and ADM) by capacity:

For example, for STM1:

$$IF \left(C39 = \textit{"check"}; \text{ then } 2 * \text{ the total number of rings adjusted to take account of B98} = \textit{"check"}; \text{ else } 2 * \text{ the total number of rings} \right)$$
$$+ \text{ the number of nodes by adjusted capacity } 2$$

- Number of regenerators:

$$\left(roundup \left(\frac{\text{RCU - LS average distance ("technical" sheet)}}{\text{average distance between regenerators ("technical" sheet)}} \right), 0 \right) - 1 * \text{ diversity of regenerators ("technical" sheet)}$$
$$* \text{ total number of physical routes}$$

The rounded function up (z,0) rounds the result of the ratio z upwards to the next integer.

Trenches

The first table recapitulates the length of trenches by geo-type (lines 7 to 10). Then the breakdown of trenches is implemented as follows:

1. Nonshared trenches (with other networks) are identified and corresponding costs allocated to the core network (lines 15 to 18).
2. Shared trenches are identified (lines 20 to 23).
3. The proportion of shared trenches costs that are attributable to the general network is then derived.
4. The model adds directly attributable costs (non-shared trenches) and indirectly attributable costs (proportion of shared trench costs) to obtain the total cost of trenches allocated to the core network.

The length of cables is calculated in terms of the number of cables declared per duct (1 by default, cell Tech C70). The length of fibers required is calculated. It is equal to the average length of the transmission routes (all geo-types considered [Tech line 22]) multiplied by the number of physical routes taken from the Capa ElTr sheet (route between two ADMs). The total obtained is then multiplied by four, assuming that each route is served by four fibers in general. By dividing the length of the fibers by the length of the cables, the average number of fibers per cable is obtained. And, from this latter information, the model determines the minimum fiber capacity of cable (6, 12, 24, 36, 48, and 96 fibers).

Microwave Network

Two cases are envisaged:

- A microwave link is used to close an SDH ring. This is usually justified when it is too costly to lay down a cable (stretches of water, mountains, crossing foreign countries).
- The transmission network has not been upgraded to SDH technology.

The closure of SDH rings is done with 155 Mbit/s systems. The non-SDH links are only recommended for narrow band systems (bandwidth inferior to 155 Mbit/s). The non-SDH links are therefore dedicated to connect areas or localities for which SDH systems are not viable. Three capacity levels are retained: 34, 8, and 2 Mbit/s.

For each type of link and technology, the model calculates:

a. The number of radio systems from the number of routes.

b. The length of the networks and the average distance of leaps.

c. The number of pylons and the breakdown of these pylons by size (light, medium, and heavy).

d. The necessary antenna equipment.

Costs

The costs are calculated on three distinct sheets: one for the switching costs (Costs Sw), one for the transmission costs (Costs Tr), and one for the infrastructure costs (Costs Infra).

At the head of each sheet, the model recapitulates the size and number of equipment planned, and information needed to allocate cost of shared equipment. The investment costs per equipment type are calculated as follows:

Investment = volume required $\star$ unit cost $\star$
(1 + installation cost (in percent)) $\star$
(1 − residual value/(1 + life span) $^\wedge$ (capital cost))

An investment annuity is calculated as follows (discount rate with or without incidence of the equipment price trend):

Annual repayment = investment / phi (life span, discount rate) where phi is the annuity function shown in appendix 1.

The final step is to calculate operating costs attributable to each network element.

These sheets are organized as follows:

Switching Costs (Costs Sw Sheet)

This sheet calculates the costs for the six types of node as shown below. Five cost headings are retained. Note that these headings are not relevant for all the nodes.

	RCU	LS	TS	ISI	CS	TS
Fixed costs of the switch						
Site cost of the switch						
Cost per line						
Cost per trunk						
Other related costs						

- There are no subscriber line costs for transit switches (TS and IS).
- There are no site costs for central stations of TDMA systems (co-localized with the switches or the RCUs).
- The cost of subscriber cards is included in cost per line.
- There is no cost for trunk in radio concentrator equipment.
- The number of equipment is derived from the Demand and Capa sheets (for two Mbit/s ports).

Transmission Costs (Costs Tr Sheet)

The transmission cost calculation is made as follows:

	RCU-LS	LS-LS	TS-TS	to ITS	CS-TS
STM 1					
STM 4					
STM 16					
STM 64					
Regenerators					
Digital cross connects					
Line termination systems STM 1					
Line termination systems STM 4					
Line termination systems STM 16					
Line termination systems STM 64					
TDM relay stations					
Domsat central station					
Domsat local station					
Switching sites					
Other related costs					

The cost headings, mentioned above, do not apply to all transmission links. For example, in the Domsat network, the central station is accounted for at the transit level, while local station costs are accounted for at the level of local exchanges. For operating costs, the repeaters and staff costs are added.

Infrastructure Costs (Costs Infra Sheet)

The following costs items are accounted for:

- Costs of cables.
- Costs of civil engineering.
- Costs of microwave systems.

The following table summarizes how these elements are taken into account:

Cable :		RCU- LS	LS- LS	TS- TS	To IS	
Cable 6 fibers	Meters					
Cable 12 fibers	Meters					
Cable 24 fibers	Meters					
Cable 36 fibers	Meters					
Cable 48 fibers	Meters					
Cable 96 fibers	Meters					
Trench						
Duct (meters) - transport alone	Urban					
	Suburban					
	Rural					
Duct (meters) - shared	Urban					
	Suburban					
	Rural					
Wireless						
Radio system		RCU- LS	LS- LS	TS- TS	To IS	CS- TS
155 Mbps	Number					
34 Mbps	Number					
8 Mbps	Number					
2 Mbps	Number					
Antenna equipment						
Wireless sites with environment						
Total number of pylons by dimension						
– Light	Number					
– Medium	Number					
– Heavy	Number					
Other related costs						

The calculations are similar to those of the other Cost sheets.

Total Costs (Tot Sheet)

The Tot sheet consolidates all the data calculated in the previous sections and calculates cost annuities for network elements used to provide interconnection services (see lines 34 to 40 of the Ucosts sheet). In doing so, one obtains for the switching and the transmission elements, respectively, the total traffic these elements carry, and therefore derives their costs. Dividing the total cost of elements of a network by the total traffic gives the unit cost per minute.

The Mobile Network Calculations

The mobile network is modeled with three types of node: MSC–MSC, MSC–BSC, and BSC–BTS. Three sheets are devoted to the intermediary calculations of the interconnection costs for originating and terminating services on the mobile network.

Capacity of the Mobile Network (Capa Mob Sheet)

The capacity of the mobile network is determined according two factors: the total traffic and the peak hour traffic. The sizing exercise is conducted for each network element.

Cost of the Mobile Network (Costs Mob Sheet)

The number of equipment required and the cost computations are carried out on the same sheet. The Cost sheet is similar in structure to the one reviewed earlier for the fixed network (number of equipment, investments, annualized costs, operating costs).

Switching		MCS	BSC	BTS
Equipment	Number			
Sites	Number			
Subscriber lines (variable)	Number			
TRX	Number			
Primary digital block (2 Mbit/s port)	Number of ports			

Microwave		MCS-MCS	MCS-BSC	BSC-BTS
Radio system				
155 Mbps	Number			
34 Mbps	Number			
8 Mbps	Number			
2 Mbps	Number			
Antenna equipment				
Microwave sites with environment				
Total number of pylons by dimension				
– rooftop	Number			
– Light	Number			
– Medium	Number			
– Heavy	Number			

Leased links		MCS-MCS	MCS-BSC	BSC-BTS
Urban	Number			
Interurban	Number			
Interurban	Km			

		MCS	BSC	BTS
Personnel	Number			
		MCS-MCS	MCS-MCS	BSC-BTS
Personnel	Number			

The calculation is thus based on:

- Exchanges equipment functions, features, number of equipment, number of subscribers, and number of installed TRXs.
- Microwave systems allowing connections of remote equipment to the exchanges.
- Capacity of leased lines.
- The number of staff operating the network.

Total Costs of the Mobile Network (Tot Mob Sheet)

The structure of the sheet is identical to that for the fixed network, apart from the fact that no system of realignment is implemented.

Appendixes

Appendix 1: Economic Cost Approach

Calculation without Taking into Account Technical Progress
The total discounted cost of using equipment for N years in the absence of technical progress is written:

$$C_N = I_0 + \sum_{n=1}^{N} \frac{f_n}{(1+i)^n} - \frac{V_N}{(1+i)^N}$$

where:
- N is the economic lifetime of the investment; n the current year.
- I_0 is the cost of the investment paid in year 0, or the discounted sum in year 0 of the investment costs if these are spread over several years.
- f_n is the operating-maintenance costs of year n, n = 1, 2,…, N; these costs are generally increasing over time, but generally the assumption is made that they are constant and equal at f_0.
- V_n is the resale value in year N (with conventionally $V_0 = I_0$).
  We write φ_i^N (phi function) function[1]:

$$\varphi_i^N = \sum_{1}^{N} \frac{1}{(1+i)^n} = \frac{(1+i)^N - 1}{i(1+i)^N}$$

As defined above, the total discounted cost of the implementation of the original investment I_0 over the period N is equal to C_N that is equivalent to: the dis-counted sum of the original investment and of the operating-maintenance costs less the discounted resale value of the equipment at N. Given the expression retained for $f_n = f_0$, we have:

$$C_N = I_0 + \sum_{1}^{N} \frac{f_0}{(1+i)^n} - \frac{V_N}{(1+i)^N}$$

$$= I_0 + f_0 \sum_{1}^{N} \frac{1}{(1+i)^n} - \frac{V_N}{(1+i)^N}$$

$$= I_0 + f_0 \varphi_i^N - \frac{V_N}{(1+i)^N}$$

It is then necessary to consider the *average annual economic cost* of implementing this investment, which corresponds to the LRAIC. To do so *the annual install-ment equivalent to the total discounted cost* is considered (that is to say, the sum which, paid annually from year 1 to year N, would enable it to be repaid).

$$X_N = \frac{C_N}{\sum_{1}^{N} \frac{1}{(1+i)^n}} = \frac{C_N}{\varphi_i^N} = \frac{I_0}{\varphi_i^N} + f_0 - \frac{V_N}{(1+i)^N} \frac{1}{\varphi_i^N}$$

$$= \frac{1}{\varphi_i^N} (I_0 - \frac{V_N}{(1+i)^N}) + f_0$$

The total annual cost is the sum of the:
- total investment less the discounted residual value, the whole discounted by phi (N,i) and

60

- the annual operating costs

The sum X_N spent every year during N years is equivalent to the cost C_N. It is equivalent to spend C_N straightaway or to spread expenditure X_N over N years.

Calculation Taking into Account Technical Progress

When the technical progress is considered, there is a need to introduce a factor capturing how the equipment is renewed over time (every N years).

$$D_N = C_N + \frac{C_N}{(1+i)^N} + \frac{C_N}{(1+i)^{2N}} + \ldots + \frac{C_N}{(1+i)^{kN}} + \ldots$$

This is the sum of a geometric series and can be written as:

$$D_N = \frac{C_N}{1 - \dfrac{1}{(1+i)^N}} = \frac{(1+i)^N C_N}{(1+i)^N - 1}$$

If this expression is related to the constant annual installment equivalent to the cost C_N, we have:

$$D_N = \frac{X_N}{i}$$

The value of the equipment during its lifetime is frequently used in economic calculations. This is justified by the need for a company to assess the valuation of the stock of equipment on a given date. What maximum price would a company be willing to pay for identical equipment (same age, same characteristics) if this equipment was lacking? In other terms, what is the opportunity cost that would be incurred by the loss of this equipment or the extra cost of anticipating its renewal by $N^\star - n$ years where $N^\star$ is its economic lifetime and n its age (*usage value* or *residual value*). This latter definition amounts to creating the fiction of a perfect secondhand market. In fact, in such a market, no businessperson would agree to buy used equipment more expensively than the net cost he/she would suffer if forced to buy new equipment prematurely, or sell equipment cheaper than the net cost it would entail to replace it.

According to this definition, the residual value of new equipment on date $n = 0$ is its purchase price. Its residual value at date $N^\star$ is nil, because the user will be indifferent to losing it. By assumption, the equipment would be replaced with identical equipment over a theoretically indefinite period. The maximum price one is ready to pay for old equipment is determined by comparing the costs obtained, either by procuring equipment of identical age or by buying new equipment straight away. More precisely, the usage value U_n is such that the discounted costs corresponding to the two possible solutions are equal:

- Payment of the price U_n in year n, operating the equipment in question from year $n + 1$ to year N, resale in N initially planned, renewal in identical fashion over an indefinite period as from year N.
- Purchase in year n of new equipment, operating during N years, then renewal in identical fashion over an indefinite period.

The usage value U_n is then the maximum that the company is ready to pay to pursue the operation with identical equipment, at the **same economic cost price** as that obtained with the equipment in question.

$$\frac{U_n}{(1+i)^n} + \sum_{k=n+1}^{N} \frac{f_k}{(1+i)^k} - \frac{V_N}{(1+i)^N} = \sum_{k=n+1}^{N} \frac{X_{N^\star}}{(1+i)^k}$$

In replacing the economic cost price by the sum of the operating costs f_k and of the economic depreciation a_k ($a_n = X_N - f_n$), we have:

$$\frac{U_n}{(1+i)^n} = \sum_{k=n+1}^{N} \frac{a_k}{(1+i)^k} + \frac{V_N}{(1+i)^N}$$

By subtracting the two consecutive years, we have:

$$\frac{U_{n-1}}{(1+i)^{n-1}} - \frac{U_n}{(1+i)^n} = \frac{a_n}{(1+i)^n} \qquad \text{otherwise,}$$

$$a_n = (1+i) \bullet U_{n-1} - U_n$$

where $(1+i)U_{n-1}$ is the discounted value in year n of the usage value U_{n-1}.

The economic depreciation is thus interpreted as a loss of discounted usage value.[2] The economic depreciation is thus an **annual cost representing the use of the capital.** More practically, this economic depreciation can be obtained by subtracting the amount of operating costs at each time n from the economic cost price.

Let us make simplifying assumptions. Suppose $V_N = 0$ and technical progress over time. If the cost of the investment decreases regularly at a rate g, then,

$$I_n = I_0 / (1 + g)^n$$

By h, we mean the composite rate defined by $(1 + h) = (1 + i) \star (1 + g)$.

Moreover, we retain operating costs constant over time, $f_n = f_0$.

In the first case, the economic depreciation is equal to the constant annual installment equivalent to the investment costs. Technical progress comes down to increasing the rate of discount i by a sum g, that is to say, taking it as equal to h.

We then have:

$$X_N = \frac{I_0}{\varphi^N_h} + f_0 \frac{\varphi^N_j}{\varphi^N_i} = \frac{I_0}{\varphi^N_h} + f_0$$

since j = i (growth of operating costs nil).

Thus, taking into account technical progress comes down to increasing the rate of remuneration of capital i by a factor g, which is the decrease in prices over the period in question.

Recurrent and Nonrecurrent Section of Debt Recovery

Once an annual economic cost C for a given service is determined, it can be recovered over a lifetime T of the productive resource. Assuming R_t, the recurrent amount recovered every year, and a nonrecurrent form R_1 recoverable in year 1.

The principle that must prevail is that the discounted sum of the R_ts increased with the nonrecurrent part R_1 be equal to the total C to be recovered, that is:

$$C = R_1 + \sum_{t=1}^{T} \frac{R_t}{(1 + i)^t}$$

In general, one accepts recovery of the specific interconnection costs (costs of co-localization, of connections between operators, and so forth) in the nonrecurrent part and the costs of network use (call origination and termination) in the recurrent part.

The model given here does not deal with specific costs.

Notes

1. Geometric sum of reason $1/(1 + i)$
If $S_n = a + a^2 + a^3 + \dots + a^n$, then we have the following equations:
$S_n - S_{n-1} = a^n$ and $a + aS_{n-1} = S_n$ and that gives:

$$S_n = a\frac{1 - a^n}{1 - a}$$

by putting $a = 1/(1 + i)$, we obtain $1 - a = ia$ and:

$$S_n = \frac{(1+i)^n - 1}{i(1+i)^n} = \frac{1}{i}(1 - \frac{1}{(1+i)^n})$$

2. If a more financial interpretation is given, the economic depreciation represents the annuity by means of which the initial investment could be repaid if it were borrowed at a rate equal to the discount rate. The nominal loss of usage value thus corresponds to the share of repayment in capital of this annuity. The usage value thus corresponds to the capital not yet repaid.

Appendix 2: Capital Cost Approach

The cost of the operators' capital must reflect the opportunity cost of the funds invested in the components of the network and the other connected assets. Traditionally it reflects the following elements:

- The average (weighted) cost of the indebtedness for the various means of financing available to each operator.
- The cost of the equity capital, measured by the return the shareholders require, to invest in the network—taking into account the risks tied to this investment.
- The value of the borrowed capital and the equity capital.

This information can then be used to determine the weighted average cost of capital (WACC) according to the following formula:

$$WACC = r_e \times E/(D + E) + r_d \times D/(D + E)$$

where r_e is the cost of the equity capital, r_d is the cost of borrowing, E is the total value of the equity capital, and D is the total value of the interest-producing debt.

The calculation of the WACC for a given operator considered globally would be relatively direct, provided possible arguments on the exact calculation and the value of the input data of the WACC formulas are set aside. Nevertheless, it may be that the regulators must establish whether the application of the global capital cost represented by the WACC is appropriate for the regulated activities of the operators; when such is the case, the global WACC could serve to determine the interconnection fees.

Otherwise, the regulators can take into account the fact that various risk premiums are normally applicable to different activities, which could translate into differences on the level of the cost of equity capital r_e, even if the financial structure is the same. In that case, there could be a different WACC for each branch of activity or each activity broken down (mobile telecommunications, cable television, or international services).

The financial economy, and the actual behavior, of investors teach that the cost of equity capital r_e is equal to the cost of borrowing without risk, to which is added a risk premium that depends on the activity invested upon, and on the financial market in demand. Activities where competition is liveliest usually entail a higher risk. The cost of borrowing r_d also varies between activities and between companies but to a lesser extent than the cost of equity capital r_e for a given financial market. As far as the structure of the capital (E and D), is concerned, it should also reflect the balance sheet of each main activity. When there is only one main balance sheet for several activities, it is acceptable to assume that these activities share the same capital structure. In this light, it can usually be assumed that the cost of borrowing r_d is the same for all activities, unless their results are judiciously different.

The WACC must be applied to a capital value for the components of the network and the other related assets, in order to determine the return to be attained, with the help of interconnection fees. While it is relatively easy to determine the value of borrowed capital and equity capital for an operator as a whole, it is not easy to determine these values for each of the operator's activities. This is because decisions on financing by borrowing are to a large extent company decisions. They are determined by various factors, such as the historical loan facilities and tax management considerations. It follows that the indebtedness of the company is liable not to correspond exactly to the financial needs of its various activities.

To fix prices, the regulators and the operators are interested in the average capital employed during a given period, rather than the capital employed at a given moment, for example, at the end of the financial year. This is justified by the fact that a "snapshot" of the situation, at a given time, will not likely represent the average level of capital committed by the operator. To be precise, the balance of working capital at a given time cannot represent the average need for liquid assets over a lengthy period. The separate operators' accounting must, therefore, indicate the average capital engaged, and not an end-of-year balance.

Accounting Values and Market Values

The great increase in the valuation of telecommunications operators in 1999–2000 raised the question of the choice of an accounting value for E (equity capital entered in the balance sheet) or of a market value (stock market capitalization). It is generally accepted that the cost of capital must reflect the minimum remuneration expected by the fund providers as a whole (shareholders and creditors). From this point of view, the E value should reflect the stock market capitalization as long as this is not the result of a speculative bubble. In fact, in this latter case, the financial markets are inefficient. Therefore, regulators and operators must agree on a sort of target financial structure where the capitalization is coherent with the expectation of future profits.

This assessment is important. In fact, the indebtedness lever (D/E relation) can be very different depending on whether an accounting value of E or a stock market value is considered; however, as re is greater than rd, this choice could exert a considerable impact on the WACC.

Effect of Profits Tax

In the WACC formula, re represents the cost required on the share capital and rd the cost of the financial debt; this is situated before tax, that is to say that $r_d = r_d$ $(1 - \theta)$, where r_d is the actuarial rate of the financial debt and q the rate of profits tax.

The use of WACC in determining tariffs is not in common use and leads to adapting it. As it is defined above, the WACC is net of tax. However, the tariff of a service is fixed before tax. It is therefore necessary to increase the WACC by the rate of profits tax and to use the corrected WACC:

$$WACC^* = \frac{r_e}{(1+\theta)} \times \frac{E}{D+E} + r_d^* \times \frac{D}{D+E}$$

where r_d^* represents the actuarial rate of the financial debt.

Appreciation of re and rd

re and rd are calculated on the basis of a reference rate called rate without risk, corresponding in general to the return on long-term (10-year) risk-free bonds (state bonds). To this rate a risk premium must be added corresponding to the activity involved and to the type of finance considered.

The risk premium may be assessed on the past fluctuations of the security, or better on the fluctuations of similar securities (sector assessment) so as to apprehend

what is called the market trend, linking the expected profitability to the level of risk. The return of the shares is then expressed as follows:

$$r_e = r_f + \beta \times (r_m - r_f)$$

where:

r_f is the risk-free return.

r_m is the average return expected on the market (for example, the return represented by a market reference index of the type of Dow Jones, S&P, CAC) (level of market return).

β is a weighting coefficient of the market differential (equity beta).

It is generally accepted that interconnection represents less risk than the fixed telephony activity, which itself represents less risk than mobile telephony. As in general a rate of return corresponding to the global activity is retained (for the reasons recalled at the start of this appendix), the risk premium tends to decrease when the interconnection activity increases.

If r_f and r_m are given by the financial market concerned, the regulator must assess the operator's beta coefficient, and adapt it, to take into account the share in its interconnection activity. β, therefore, measures an elasticity of the sensitivity of the operator's security to variations in the market index: if the profitability of the market varies by 1 point, the profitability of the security varies by b points. In the African context, telecommunications operators are generally considered as less risky values than the average value of the market: β is therefore generally lower than 1.

As far as r_d^* is concerned, it is generally calculated as the risk-free return to which a premium (spread or debt premium) specific to the operator concerned is added. This return can be assessed either on the basis of the market values (risk-free return plus premium) or on the basis of contractual values presented by the operator (annual average weighted cost of the operator's indebtedness)

Thus, the WACC taken into account in the model is expressed as follows:

$$WACC^* = \frac{r_f + \beta \times (r_m - r_f)}{(1+\theta)} \times \frac{E}{D+E} + (r_f + s_p) \times \frac{D}{D+E}$$

To calculate it, therefore, we need:

- $D/(D + E)$, share of the debt on the total financial structure (which enables us to deduce $E/(D + E)$; this ratio is sometimes called the level of gearing or leverage.
- r_f, risk-free return of the financial market considered.
- r_m, average return of the financial market considered (expected growth of the reference stock market index).
- β, risk note of the security.
- s_p, risk premium of the operator.
- θ, rate of profits tax.

These six values are required to calculate the WACC. By default, values are proposed. For more details on the application of these concepts, refer to Alexander and others (1999).

Appendix 3: Radio Concentrator Solutions

Today, there are only a small number of TDMA technology radio concentrator manufacturers. In fact, the purchase of Lucent TRT by SRT, the giving up of such solutions by the majors such as Alcatel or Siemens, means that SRT and NEC and a few small constructors from low-density countries (Australia) remain the last suppliers of these technologies, which are now challenged by other solutions (fixed global system mobile, satellite, and so forth).

Radio concentrators are particularly suitable for low-density rural zones with wide gaps between each village. They enable subscribers far from the exchange (up to 1,600 km) to be connected, and can tolerate constraints specific to rural areas (for example, electric power provided by solar panels). A leap between stations can be up to 50 km.

These systems can operate in the 500 MHz, 1.5 GHz, 2.5 GHz, and 3.5 GHz bands. The last leap can be by wire or else wireless thanks to a wireless local loop termination. These systems offer basic telephone and public phone services, group 3 fax, data transmission services as well as basic Integrated system digital network (2B+D) services. They use TDMA distribution, which enables the available spectrum to be optimized. The nodal and remote stations connected only use one frequency pair. They often use Yagi antennas.

The capacity of these systems can go up to 4,096 subscribers and traffic of 188 E. It should be noted that these calculations are carried out for a loss rate of 1 percent. In fact, the traffic capacity is greater because local calls do not use resources. Two subscribers connected to the same station can communicate without occupying a channel.

The **central station (CS)** connects to the splitter of the automatic exchange of the public network. The CS is linked by microwave to the remote stations. The radio subassembly may be deported and linked by cable or radio at 2 Mbit/s.

The repeater station (RS) serves as a relay between sites not seen by the central station. The repeater station can provide up to 120 circuits at 64 kbit/s or 240 circuits at 32 kbit/s.

The **terminal station (TS;** SDE on the diagram) connects the subscribers. The terminal station can connect cabled subscribers or those with a DECT solution.

Figure A3.1 Example of the Architecture of an IRT (TRT-Lucent Network)

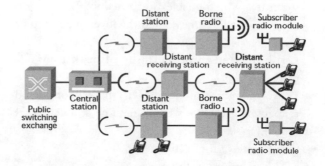

Table A3.1 Number of Subscribers Depending on the Traffic per Subscriber (in mE)

Traffic per subscriber	Number of subscribers
50	1024
60	850
70	700
80	650
90	600
100	520
110	500
120	470
130	450
140	420
150	400

Note: It is assumed that 30 percent of calls are local; otherwise, the system loses between 5 percent and 15 percent of its subscribers.

Bibliography

The word *processed* describes informally reproduced works that may not be commonly available through libraries.

Alexander, I., A. Estache, A. Oliveri. 1999. "A Few Things Transport Regulators Should Know about Risk and the Cost of Capital." The World Bank Institute. Processed.

Armstrong, M. 1998. "Network Interconnection in Telecommunications." *Economic Journal* 108:545–64.

Armstrong, M., C. Doyle, and J. Vickers. 1996. "The Access Pricing Problem: A Synthesis." *Journal of Industrial Economics* 44:131–50.

Armstrong, M., and J. Vickers. 1998. "The Access Pricing Problem with Deregulation: A Note." *Journal of Industrial Economics* 46:115–21.

Benitez, D., A. Estache, M. Kennett, and C. Ruzzier. 2000. "Are Cost Models Useful for Telecoms Regulators in Developing Countries?" Policy Research Working Paper 2384. The World Bank Institute.

BIPE. 2000. "What Telecom Regulation for Low-Income African Countries?" Study for the European Commission. Available at http://europa.eu.int/ISPO/intcoop/i_acp.html.

BIPE. 2003. Field Units Reports: Cameroon, Côte d'Ivoire, Zambia, Burkina Faso.

Celani, M. O. D. Petrecolla, and C. A. Ruzzier. 2002. "Desagregación de redes en telecomunicaciones. Una visión desde la política de defensa de la competencia." Processed.

Economides, N. 1996. "The Economics of Networks." *International Journal of Industrial Organization* 14:673–99.

———. 1998. "The Incentive for Non-Price Discrimination by an Input Monopolist." *International Journal of Industrial Organization* 16:271–84.

Economides, N., and L. J. White. 1995. "Access and Interconnection Pricing: How Efficient Is the 'Efficient Component Pricing Rule'?" *Antitrust Bulletin* 40:557–79.

Hausman, J. 1996. "Reply Affidavit of Prof. Jerry Hausman, FCC CC Docket No. 96-98" and "Valuation and the Effect of Regulation on New Services in Telecommunications." Brookings Papers on Economic Activity: Microeconomics.

Jamison, M. 1998. "Regulatory Techniques for Addressing Interconnection, Access, and Cross-Subsidy in Telecommunications." In Margaret Arblaster and Mark A. Jamison, eds., *Infrastructure Regulation and Market Reform: Principles and Practice.* Australian Competition and Consumer Commission and the Public Utility Research.

———. 1999. "Does Practice Follow Principle? Applying Real Options Principles To Proxy Costs in U.S. Telecommunications." In James Alleman and Eli Noam, eds., *Real Options: The New Investment Theory and its Implications for Telecommunications Economics.* Boston: Kluwer Academic Publishers.

Laffont, J. J. 1998. "Translating Principles into Practice." EDI Regulatory Reform Discussion Paper. World Bank, Washington, D.C. http://www.worldbank.org/wbi/regulation/wp.htm.

Laffont, J. J., and J. Tirole. 1996. "Creating Competition through Interconnection: Theory and Practice." *Journal of Regulatory Economics* 10:227–56.

———. 2001. *Competition in Telecommunications.* Munich Lectures, The MIT Press, 2nd ed.

Laffont, J. J., P. Rey, and J. Tirole. 1998. "Network Competition: I. Overview and Non-discriminatory Pricing; II. Discriminatory Pricing." *RAND Journal of Economics* 29:1–56.

Salinger, M. 1998. "Regulating Prices to Equal Forward Looking Costs: Cost-Based Prices or Price-Based Costs?" *Journal of Regulatory Economics* 14:149–64.

Sidak, J. G., and D. Spulber. 1997. "The Tragedy of the Telecommons: Government Pricing of Unbundled Network Elements under the Telecommunications Act of 1996." *Columbia Law Review* 71:1081–161.

Spulber, D., and J. G. Sidak. 1997. "Network Access Pricing and Deregulation." *Industry and Corporate Change* 6:757–82.

Valletti, T. 1998. "The Practice of Access Pricing: Telecoms in the UK." The World Bank, EDIRP. Processed.

———. 2001. "The Theory of Access Pricing and Its Linkage with Investment Incentives." In Martin Cave, Papers on Access Pricing Investment and Entry in Telecommunications. Warwick Business School, Research paper series.

Valletti, T., and A. Estache. 1998. "The Theory of Access Pricing: An Overview for Infrastructure Regulators." The World Bank Institute. Available at http://www.worldbank.org/wbi/regulation/wp.htm.

Wildman, S. S. 1997. "Interconnection Pricing, Stranded Costs, and the Optimal Regulatory Contract." *Industrial and Corporate Change* 6:741–55.